THE DOMINICAN REPUBLIC

NATIONS OF CONTEMPORARY LATIN AMERICA
Ronald Schneider
General Editor

† *Nicaragua: The Land of Sandino*, Thomas W. Walker

Honduras, James A. Morris

† *Mexico: Profile of Stable Development*, Daniel Levy and Gabriel Szekely

Paraguay, Riordan Roett

† *The Dominican Republic: A Caribbean Crucible*, Howard J. Wiarda and Michael J. Kryzanek

Also of Interest

† *The End and the Beginning: The Nicaraguan Revolution*, John A. Booth

† *Latin American Foreign Policies: Global and Regional Dimensions*, edited by Elizabeth G. Ferris and Jennie K. Lincoln

† *The Continuing Struggle for Democracy in Latin America*, edited by Howard J. Wiarda

† *Authoritarian Capitalism: Brazil's Contemporary Economic and Political Development*, edited by Thomas C. Bruneau and Philippe Faucher

Corporatism and National Development in Latin America, Howard J. Wiarda

† *From Dependency to Development: Strategies to Overcome Underdevelopment and Inequality*, edited by Heraldo Muñoz

† *Post-Revolutionary Peru: The Politics of Transformation*, edited by Stephen M. Gorman

† *Revolution in El Salvador: Origins and Evolution*, Tommie Sue Montgomery

† Available in hardcover and paperback.

THE DOMINICAN REPUBLIC

A Caribbean Crucible

Howard J. Wiarda
Michael J. Kryzanek

Westview Press / Boulder, Colorado

The paper used in this publication meets the requirements of the American National Standard for Permanence of Paper for Printed Library Materials Z39.48-1984.

Nations of Contemporary Latin America

Photograph credits: all pictures except the four listed below were taken by Warren Smith and are published through the courtesy of Public Affairs Analysts, Inc. Chapter 3, Independence Park photo courtesy of Milton T. Cole; Chapter 5, university building photo courtesy of Jueves 68; Chapter 7, Balaguer photo courtesy of United Press International, and Guzmán photo courtesy of Jacques Lowe. All are published by permission.

Published in 1982 in the United States of America by
Westview Press, Inc.
5500 Central Avenue
Boulder, Colorado 80301
Frederick A. Praeger, Publisher

Library of Congress Cataloging in Publication Data
Wiarda, Howard J., 1939-
The Dominican Republic, a Caribbean crucible.
(Nations of contemporary Latin America)
Bibliography: p.
Includes index.
1. Dominican Republic. I. Kryzanek, Michael J. II. Title. III. Series.
F1934.W49   972.93   81-16421
ISBN O-89158-977-5   AACR2
ISBN O-86531-333-4 (pbk.)

Printed and bound in the United States of America

10   9   8   7   6   5   4

For our parents
John and the late Cornelia Wiarda
and
Edward and Mary Kryzanek

in loving appreciation
for all the help along the way

Contents

Illustrations

Foreword

Although no single country is truly "typical" of the diverse region we are accustomed to calling Latin America, a few do come close to approximating the norm. In a very fundamental sense this is what makes the Dominican Republic fascinating for the comparativist. Subtract the major Latin American states – Brazil, Mexico, and Argentina – and this larger half of a Caribbean island becomes quite representative of the twenty-odd nations remaining. Certainly most of their problems and contradictions can be found in the Dominican Republic, albeit perhaps differing in scale and intensity. Thus during the past generation the Dominican Republic has experienced both the highly institutionalized authoritarian rule of the Trujillo regime – the first in this hemisphere to really merit the label "totalitarian" – and significant experiments with broad, participatory political democracy. Developments in the last quarter century alone have included nearly every major variation between these poles: a populist *caudillo*, radical reformism, several regimes based on elite manipulation, and even civil war and foreign intervention. No wonder, then, that Dominican reality has been portrayed in widely differing terms depending not only on the political flood tide of the moment, but also upon the ideological commitment of the particular analysts.

It is within this context that a profile of "a Caribbean Crucible" takes on special significance as one of the most important case studies constituting our series on the nations of contemporary Latin America. No single conventional approach is suitable or sufficient for the entire range of Latin American experience, and none is appropriate for this complex little country alone. The authors have accepted the challenge of understanding the Dominican Republic on its own terms, then explaining it to a foreign readership in terms that will be meaningful. The authors have also successfully portrayed both the individuality of this country and its comparable features; in so doing they have set a high standard for other analysts to follow. Indeed, the conceptualization framing this inquiry reflects Professor Wiarda's well-deserved reputation as a leading theorist of Latin American development, for he is a creative synthesizer as well as a persuasive exponent of a most sophisticated and sensitive type of cultural relativism. Dr. Kryzanek contributes a perceptive familiarity with the nuances of Dominican culture and society as well as with the present-day political scene.

In sum, all the actors of Latin American political drama are present in the Dominican story, along with many of the elements of tragedy. Clearly, racial tensions, the role of multinational corporations, and friction with neighboring countries – all treated with balance and insight in this study – are among the factors that make the Dominican Republic a microcosm of the Caribbean and Central America, if not of all Latin America. Yet even beyond the normal patterns for this region, the Dominican Republic, in its long colonial experience and relatively short life as an independent nation, has been subject to a series of intense international pressures going back to sixteenth-, seventeenth-, and eighteenth-century conflicts among the imperial powers of Europe and their subsequent reflections during and after the Napoleonic Wars. In the present century the buffeted national life of the Dominican Republic reflects more clearly than in any other country all the key shifts in U.S. policy toward Latin America. Perhaps Wilson, Roosevelt, Kennedy, Johnson, and even Carter have left as lasting a mark upon Dominican history as they have upon their own country. This fact further accentuates the importance of this particular volume to an appreciation of the actual Latin American situation.

Ronald M. Schneider

Preface

The Dominican Republic has or has had everything a reader or student of Latin America might look for: romance, high adventure, exciting history, perhaps the world's most oppressive dictatorship, a heroic struggle for democracy, repeated American interventions, rapacious multinationals, revolutionary politics, class struggle, and infinitely complex racial and social relations. In addition, the Dominican Republic lies close to Cuba, close to the United States, and at the center of the storms and the fire stirring throughout the Caribbean. The Dominican Republic is a microcosm of the immense changes sweeping all of Latin America and the Third World, a test case, a crucible of the issues and wrenching conflicts of the development process.

The Dominican Republic's importance is actually out of proportion to its size, population, or resources. Though a small country, historically neglected, beaten, and exploited, it has retained its sense of pride and dignity and is seeking a proper formula for organizing its political, social, and economic life. Certainly that formula will contain elements borrowed from the United States and other already developed nations, but what we find particularly exciting is the Dominicans' efforts to develop an indigenous, Dominican model of development rather than some pale imitation of the "Western" mode. This process implies that the Dominican Republic can no longer be viewed as a less-developed version of the United States, certain to emulate us and follow our path to modernization; rather it must be looked at in its own context and on its own increasingly nationalistic terms.

The search for its own proper destiny, a framework for national modernization based not on inappropriate foreign models but on its own traditions, institutions, and culture, is, in the Dominican Republic as elsewhere in the Third World, still incomplete. However, the search itself is exciting and the fact that the Dominicans have begun it indicates an effort to break out of their historic patterns of dependency, inferiority, and underdevelopment. The long-term implications of these changes are enormous – and not just for the Dominicans!

The authors of this book have been studying the Dominican Republic for a considerable period, going back to the early 1960s in one case and to the early 1970s in the other. Between us, we have visited or lived in the country on fourteen separate occasions, and in the twenty-odd years since we began studying the Dominican Republic, we have spent at least some time in the country during more than three-quarters of those years. Both of us have written extensively about the Dominican Republic in other formats, but those studies are now either out of date or out of print. No other study exists that provides an up-to-date, comprehensive overview of Dominican national life.

The authors would like to thank those countless Dominicans who, in formal interviews or in numerous briefer encounters, have helped us to understand their country. Thanks are also due our wives and children – Carol and Iêda, Laura and Kathryn, and Kristy, Howard, and Jonathan – who have given up conversations and companionship, as well as backyard baseball games, for the sake of this book. Special thanks are due Kristy Lynn Wiarda, who, as a *Dominicana* born in Santo Domingo in 1964 and now interested in her "roots," read and commented upon the entire manuscript. Lynne Rienner has been an especially attentive publisher, one of the few left who are actually interested in themes and ideas. Our thanks also go to Ms. Joni Corsini, who cheerfully provided us with her typing skills. The usual disclaimers apply, absolving those named of culpability and placing all responsibility for the book's contents on the authors.

Howard J. Wiarda
Michael J. Kryzanek

Abbreviations

AID	Agency for International Development
CARICOM	Caribbean Common Market
CDE	Dominican Electric Power Corporation
CEDOPEX	Dominican Center for Promotion of Exports
CFI	Industrial Development Corporation
FED	Dominican Student Federation
FIDE	Investment Fund for Economic Development
IAD	Dominican Agrarian Institute
IADB	Inter-American Development Bank
IAPF	Inter-American Peace Force
IDECOOP	Institute for Cooperative Development and Credit
ILO	International Labor Organisation
INDOTEC	Dominican Institute of Industrial Technology
INESPRE	Price Stabilization Institute
INFRATUR	(tourism infrastructure projects)
LAFTA	Latin American Free Trade Association
MPD	Dominican Popular Movement
OAS	Organization of American States
ODC	Office of Community Development
OPIC	Overseas Private Investment Corporation
PCD	Dominican Communist Party
PLD	Party of Dominican Liberation
PQD	Partido Quisqueyano Dominicano
PRD	Dominican Revolutionary Party
UASD	Autonomous University of Santo Domingo
UCN	National Civic Union
UN	United Nations

1

Introduction

The importance of the Dominican Republic as a significant and influential member of the Latin American community of nations has seldom been recognized. Attention ebbs and flows, but most of it has been devoted to the larger and more populous countries of the area: those that are oil-rich or whose revolutions make dramatic headlines. The Dominican Republic, barely the size of South Carolina and with a population of approximately five million, has frequently been overshadowed by countries whose natural resources, demographic figures, or internal politics put them in the spotlight of international attention.

The Dominican Republic may not hold the answer to the "mystery" of Latin America. Nor can it always compete for attention and notoriety with Argentina, Brazil, Chile, Cuba, or Mexico. Nevertheless, the Dominican Republic is an important nation, strategically located in the vortex of the Caribbean hurricane, a weather vane and direction pointer within the area. Dominican intellectual and former president Juan Bosch has written a book discussing the Caribbean as an "imperial frontier" during the past five hundred years, with the Dominican Republic at its center; and at least since the time of President Polk, the United States has been interested in the strategic importance of the island, paying close attention to both its international connections and its internal politics. And, as stated in our preface, the Dominican Republic has had virtually everything the student of Latin American affairs might look for: great drama, conflict, and change.

The Dominican Republic is in many respects a microcosm of the entire area. Within this small nation's borders and throughout its history it is possible to see all the wrenching divisions, developmental dilemmas, crises, and controversies characteristic of Latin America. The country has endured repeated interventions by foreign powers, of which the United States, from 1916 to 1924 and 1965 to 1966, is only the most recent. It continues to balance precariously between its strongly authoritarian traditions on the one hand and its democratic tradition on the other, now complicated by the presence of various socialist strains. It has to cope with the vicious circles of underdevelopment and the anxiety of a

1

one-crop (sugar) dependent economy. It experiences the social upheavals and conflict precipitated by immense class differences and accelerated social change, and the perpetual political tensions generated by the claims of rival elites who have largely incompatible views of how these problems should be met.

The Dominican Republic is not only a "central depository" of all that is Latin American, but has also been a "living laboratory" for new social and political experiments. It has had its order-and-progress dictators, its periods of republican rule alternating with modernizing tyrannies, its eras of populism and change, a bloody revolution and civil war in 1965 that led to U.S. intervention, a time of capitalist development, and is now experiencing thrusts toward socialism and social democracy. In short, the Dominican Republic has often been a pacesetter for the rest of Latin America, both for good and for ill – a nation that has been a proving ground and, when the U.S. Marines landed, an alarm system. In the process, it has been the focus of numerous hemispheric conflicts in recent decades.

The Dominican Republic has frequently provided a fascinating preview of important shifts in the directions of Latin American political change and of U.S. policy toward the area. In 1905 the Dominican Republic provided the world with a first glimpse of the infamous "Roosevelt Corollary" to the Monroe Doctrine, under which the United States forcibly intervened in at least a half-dozen Latin American countries. In the regime of Rafael Trujillo, the Dominican Republic produced one of the world's longest-lived and most tightly knit dictatorships, whose bloody rule increased our understanding of authoritarian and totalitarian control but was not very pleasant for many Dominicans. Trujillo's rule also provides an interesting case study of how the United States bolsters dictators who support its policies, and then moves to undermine and, in this case, even assassinate them when they have outlived their usefulness.

For a time the Dominican Republic was the showcase for the ill-fated American aid program known as the Alliance for Progress. It was also in the Dominican Republic that the showcase shattered and the Alliance collapsed – first when Juan Bosch's democratic government was overthrown in 1963, and then definitively in 1965 when the United States sent its Marines to crush a Bosch-led democratic revolution. The American intervention there was a prelude to its even more massive intervention in Viet Nam, and signalled to the rest of Latin America that the United States would not permit revolutionary change in what it considered its sphere of influence. In 1978, however, the United States intervened again, this time diplomatically instead of militarily, to enable an elected Dominican social-democratic government to take power, rather than be overthrown by a military coup even before its inauguration.

In sum, there can be no doubt of the Dominican Republic's importance or of its role as a beacon signalling the way of hemispheric changes and of U.S.-Latin American relations. As a strategically located island, its significance cannot be measured in square miles or oil barrels, and as a frequent pacesetter in the hemisphere with innovative social and political experiments, this "laboratory's" influence stretches beyond mere economic, geographic, or demographic numbers.

To introduce the Dominican Republic as innovator and bellwether, and as having strategic significance beyond its size, is to miss some other of its essential strengths, which makes it even more crucial that we give it our attention. The fact is that the Dominican Republic is a fascinating country in its own right. It has been struggling for nearly five hundred years, against foreign occupiers and internal chaos, to establish its own institutional framework for development. Historically characterized by a lack of institutions—feudal or capitalist, conservative or liberal—the Dominican Republic has struggled valiantly to fill this organizational void. Whether this struggle will succeed, precisely what form its institutions will take, whether it is possible to blend outside influences and indigenous traditions—all these are still unknown. Only one thing is certain: the forms that are devised, the group and personal interrelations, the policy processes, and the habits of behavior and cultural patterns will be typically Dominican.

The profile of the Dominican Republic that is presented here will thus seek to explore the country from a number of vantage points. Chapter 2 will provide a general overview of the land, the culture, and the people, with special emphasis on the changing character of life in the Dominican Republic. Chapters 3 and 4 will describe the historical evolution of the country from the Spanish conquest to contemporary times. Chapters 5, 6, and 7 will be concerned, respectively, with the major social, economic, and political features of the country as well as the interrelationships of social class structure, economic dependency and underdevelopment, and political power. Chapters 8 and 9 will center on the key issues of policy and policy making in both the domestic and the international arenas, focusing on the Dominican Republic's developmental options and its crucial relations with the United States.

Woven together throughout these chapters are a number of unifying threads and themes. These include an emphasis on the Dominican Republic's strategic and political importance and its position as a pacesetter, a microcosm, a *crucible* of Latin American social and political change. We shall insist on viewing the Dominican Republic in the light of its own history and cultural traditions, and not from the frequently ethnocentric and biased viewpoint of the United States or Western Europe. We shall be concerned both with Dominican internal politics and economics and with its external dependency and interrelations with a broader world. Finally, we shall look sympathetically on the Dominican Republic's efforts to find its own place in the sun, to break out of its vicious circles of underdevelopment, to devise a more democratic political system – albeit democracy derived from its own traditions – to establish its position within a Caribbean region that is turbulent now and certain to become even more so in the near future.

Our study of the Dominican Republic seeks to weave these diverse themes together so the complete profile that is presented captures the distinctiveness of that country as well as its broader importance for understanding Caribbean, Latin American, and Third World contexts. We hope that the picture we draw will help others comprehend, with empathy and understanding, this land of beauty and misery, of richness and poverty, of hope and tragedy, of dreams lost and realized, and yet of abiding dignity, perseverance, and aspiration.

2

The Land, the People, the Culture

In 1492, when Columbus first sighted what is today the Dominican Republic, he reported to Spain that he had found a land that was "the fairest under the sun." Nestled in the chain of Caribbean islands between Cuba and Puerto Rico, the Dominican Republic, with its fertile valleys and plateaus, its favorable climate and gentle winds (except during hurricane season), its docile natives and considerable mineral wealth, was the favored early location for the seat of Spanish trade, culture, and administration in the New World. As proof of Columbus's love for the island and its importance in the early Spanish colonial empire, he named it "Española" (later Anglicized to "Hispaniola"), or "Little Spain."

THE LAND

The island of Hispaniola today is divided into two countries: the Dominican Republic, which is Hispanic, Western, Spanish-speaking, and predominantly white or mulatto; and Haiti, which is French and African culturally (though often with a thin veneer of Westernism), French- or *patois*-speaking (patois is a native dialect), and predominantly black. The Dominican Republic occupies the eastern two thirds (19,386 square miles or 48,464 square kilometers) of Hispaniola, stretching from the mountainous regions in the north and west of the island to the eastern coast that looks out toward Puerto Rico. Haiti has about the same population in half as much territory. In history, culture, language, and racial attitudes, the two neighbors on Hispaniola have little in common. Nor have the relations between them often been friendly.

The Haitian countryside is barren, impoverished, largely denuded of vegetation, with most of its topsoil washed away – a potential "basket case" with all the attendant horrors of disaster and mass starvation. The Dominican Republic is lush, tropical, with rich vegetation. Travelers to the latter country consistently marvel at both the beauty and diversity of

5

6

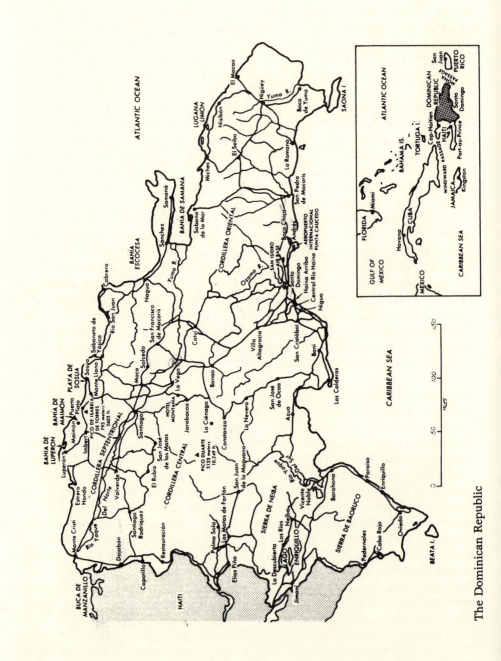

The Dominican Republic

the topographical and climatic conditions. The Dominican countryside is a mixture of mountain ranges, semiarid deserts, rich farmlands, tropical rain forests, and picture-post-card beaches. Geographers who have studied the Dominican Republic call it one of the most diverse countries in the world with over twenty distinct geographic regions that can be identified.

Dominating the central area of the country are the mountain ranges, or *cordilleras*. The Dominican Republic has four parallel mountain ranges running from northwest to southeast, chopping up the country into smaller segments and separating the capital city of Santo Domingo on the Southern coast from the rich agricultural heartland in the Vega Real (the "Royal Plain") and from the center of the country's burgeoning tourist trade on the northern coast.

The mountain ranges, although majestic and beautiful, are largely unpopulated and are perhaps less important to the Dominican Republic than the valleys lying between these "fingers" of the cordillera. In the northern part of the country, surrounding the Dominican Republic's second largest city of Santiago, is the Cibão Valley. The Cibão is often referred to as the bread basket of the country because of its production of grains, beef cattle, and export commodities such as tobacco.

Although the valleys of the northern cordilleras contain rich farming and grazing areas, in the southwest the valleys are semiarid deserts unsuitable to agriculture and with some of the poorest people to be found in the country. At the eastern end of the island the cordillera gives way to a plain of over one thousand square miles (2,590 sq. km.), much of it owned by the Gulf and Western Corporation. It is a region of seemingly endless sugar cane fields, yielding the primary export commodity of the country. Surrounding the entire country are some of the loveliest and, until recently, most undeveloped beaches in the world.

The topographical diversity is reflected in considerable climatic diversity. The mountain areas are clear and cool, the plains and valleys warmer and more humid. But in general the climate is temperate and more pleasant than in other tropical areas. The trade winds, high elevations, and surrounding ocean help keep the average temperature at 75 degrees year round. Rainfall is moderate except on the Samana Peninsula in the northeast part of the island and in the mountain areas around Santiago, where as much as one hundred inches (254 centimeters) per year may fall. The remainder of the country usually enjoys clear, sunny days with only an occasional afternoon or nighttime shower.

Although generally blessed with favorable temperatures and rainfall, the island has serious climatic problems as well. Hispaniola lies in the "hurricane channel." A killer hurricane devastated the capital in 1930, leaving thousands dead and many more thousands homeless, and

Mountain roads in the Dominican Republic

served as a way by which Dominican dictator Rafael Trujillo justified even stronger authoritarian rule. In 1978, Hurricane David swept through the country killing more thousands and causing over $1 billion in damages – it was a storm from which the country still has not recovered. The Dominicans have also had to endure periodic droughts that have ruined the all-important sugar crop and caused severe water shortages, and they suffer almost yearly flooding as poor drainage and river control systems have left certain areas constantly susceptible to the effects of excessive rainfall.

Despite the specter of hurricanes, droughts, and floods, climatic and topographical conditions are generally favorable to agriculture, which is still the backbone of the economy, the principal employer, and the chief source of export earnings. The Dominican Republic is one of the world's leading producers of sugar, a crop that shapes not only the nation's economy but also its sociology and politics. Approximately half of the country's export earnings derive from sugar. Coffee, tobacco, cocoa, bananas, tomatoes, and other fruits are also produced for export. Agriculture thus remains the basis of the national economy, requiring stable markets and adequate prices for its continued viability.

The heavy dependence of the Dominicans on sugar and other staple crops in a world of unstable prices, however, has stimulated efforts at economic diversification, especially in the areas of mining and manufacturing. In recent years the Dominican government has permitted foreign mining concerns to search for and extract for export bauxite, nickel, gypsum, gold, oil, and copper. The ferronickel industry near the city of Bonao has been especially successful and now provides nearly 15 percent of the government's revenues. The Dominican gold industry has also advanced quickly. With skyrocketing gold prices and a vast potential for mining and production, the Dominican Republic is fast becoming one of the world's leading suppliers of this precious metal.

The effort to diversify the Dominican economy has also led to a major expansion of the tourist industry. Passed over for years by foreigners because of its unstable conditions, the Dominican Republic in the 1970s blossomed into one of the Caribbean's leading vacation spots. New hotels and tourist facilities are sprouting along both the southern and northern coasts, and the government has pledged both funds and a major publicity campaign to attract tourists. The rationale behind this campaign is not just to bring sorely-needed foreign currency into the country, but also to stimulate employment. Tourism is labor-intensive, and in a nation that suffers from chronic unemployment and underemployment, tourism means money and jobs.

Business, commerce, and industry are also growing in the Dominican Republic. Over the past thirty years, as economic growth has accelerated, new industries (cement, plastics, textiles, construction, and a great variety of others) have been established, along with an increase in commerce, banking, and entrepreneurial activities. This has led to a greater diversification of the economy, a greater concentration of the wealth and power in Santo Domingo, and a country that is no longer a "sleepy banana (or sugar) republic," but rather one that is dynamic and fast-changing.

The changing character of the economy from predominantly agricultural to one increasingly more diversified has had a major impact on the country's demography. Today, for the first time, more people live in urban than rural areas. The influx of people to the two largest cities, Santo Domingo and Santiago, has been immense. The population of the capital increased from 820,000 in 1970 to 1,200,000 in 1980. Sizable increases have also occurred in such smaller cities as La Romana, Bonao, and Puerto Plata, reflecting their respective sugar, mining, and tourism booms. The overall population has climbed from four million in 1970 to over five million in 1980.

The influx of people to the cities has created new problems and tensions as the newcomers compete for jobs and insufficient housing, services, and essentials such as water. The shantytown *barrios* around Santo Domingo often have no electricity, no real streets, no running water, and no sewage facilities. Yet life in the city is still preferable to that in the impoverished countryside, so the urban migration continues.

LIFE IN THE DOMINICAN CITY

Almost half the Dominican population still lives in the *campo* ("countryside"), often eking out a meager subsistence, living in huts made of mud, sticks, and thatch. Many work as peasants, tenants, or sharecroppers, cast with their families into a life of poverty, misery, illiteracy (about 40 percent of the population), and malnutrition. It is clear that the future lies elsewhere. To more and more Dominicans fleeing the wretched poverty of the campo, that future lies in the cities. Perhaps the changing society and demography of the Dominican Republic can be understood best by examining life in four representative cities: Santo Domingo, Santiago, La Romana, and Bonao.

Santo Domingo

The capital of the country since 1496, when Bartholomew Columbus (Christopher's brother) founded it, Santo Domingo is in nearly all respects the center of the country. Not only is it the seat of national power and administration, but it is also the hub of financial and business activity, the chief location of the country's thriving middle class, the site

New apartments in Santo Domingo

of the largest institution of higher learning, and the center of cultural attractions that include art galleries, libraries, museums, and concert halls. Socially, politically, and financially, Santo Domingo is "where the action is," which explains its tremendous recent growth. If the Dominican Republic can be characterized as a city-state-sized nation, then Santo Domingo, the primary city, is its focal point.

Santo Domingo has a history unmatched by any other in Latin America. As Spain's first administrative capital in the New World, it was the site of the first hospital, first monastery, first cathedral, and first university. The city has survived devastating hurricanes, swashbuckling pirates, numerous foreign occupations, and destructive civil wars. Yet, centered on a promontory overlooking the blue Caribbean, it retains its beauty, dignity, and sense of history.

As with any capital city, Santo Domingo is alive with activity and reflects the changes in Dominican society and economics. The "old city," with its cobblestone streets, open-air markets, small shops and craftsmen, is gradually giving way to new suburban housing and supermarkets on the outskirts of town. Construction is booming as Dominican and foreign interests recognize the importance of the capital as a business, industrial, and tourist center.

Among the more exciting aspects of life in Santo Domingo for the

George Washington Boulevard, Santo Domingo

visitor are the restoration efforts undertaken by the national government. Beginning in the early 1970s, large sections of the old city were tastefully restored to their colonial state. The cornerstone of this effort is the Alcazar de Colon, the first castle in the New World built by Columbus's son Diego.

Behind this facade of wealth and beauty, however, is the other face of Santo Domingo. The capital is also the home of hundreds of thousands of poor, unemployed, and increasingly desperate and angry people who have been bypassed by the new wealth and prosperity they see all around. The poor barrios of Santo Domingo serve as a stark reminder to all that the economic advances of the past decade are uneven and benefit but a small percentage of the total population. It is from these poor barrios that the "shock troops" for some future Dominican revolution will likely come.

Santiago

Overshadowed by the growth and dynamism of Santo Domingo is Santiago, the country's second largest city (once its largest). Often referred to by its full Spanish name of Santiago de los Caballeros ("Santiago of the Gentlemen"), this city of four hundred thousand, in the heart of the

Central Market in Santo Domingo

Cibão Valley, has traditionally been recognized as the country's agricultural center. Santiago is home to a number of the country's wealthy aristocrats and historic families and, as a result, has a reputation as a center of culture and refinement that local residents often prefer to the brashness, noise, and money-grubbing of Santo Domingo.

Although Santiago is a growing city and attracting new commercial and industrial concerns to complement its agricultural base, the city continues to be defined in terms of a handful of key, closely interrelated families, who for generations have controlled the politics and economics of both the region and the nation. Family names with deep historical roots in Dominican history like Cáceres, Espaillat, Grullón, Taváres, Cabral, and now Guzmán, are the heart of the social oligarchy of Santiago.

Because of the influence of this aristocracy, politics in Santiago and its surrounding countryside have remained more traditional and conservative than in Santo Domingo. Separated by one hundred miles from the capital's frenzy and sprawl, Santiago remains a city of relative quiet and serenity. In many respects Santiago is an important counterforce to the political, social, and economic climate of Santo Domingo. While Santo Domingo is alive with the dynamics of capitalism, boom times, and class and partisan conflict, Santiago remains almost feudal in its age-old relationships—more tranquil, stable, traditional.

La Romana

La Romana, a provincial capital, is probably the best example of a medium-sized city that has been profoundly changed by two of the most important components of Dominican national development: sugar and foreign investment. Situated on the southern coast toward the eastern end of the island, La Romana is the center of the sugar industry. A city of one hundred thousand, La Romana has the country's largest sugar refinery. Owned and operated by a Gulf and Western subsidiary, the sugar industry of La Romana churns out the bulk of the sugar exported by the country.

The story of La Romana and sugar is incomplete without mentioning the role of the giant multinational that dominates the area. Gulf and Western came to La Romana in the early 1960s. Since that time its investment has grown to over $200 million, encompassing cattle, cement, factories, and tourist hotels, as well as sugar. The impact on La Romana has been major. Its population and attendant social problems have grown enormously. But Gulf and Western has spent an estimated $20 million in making the city "the showcase of the East." Schools, churches, clinics, parks, recreation centers and employee houses have all gone up with Gulf and Western money. Gulf and Western has literally rebuilt the city.

However, there is a darker side to this picture. To run its operations, Gulf and Western has employed tough and brutal administrators from the days of the bloody dictator Batista in Cuba. Allegedly, it has bribed Dominican politicians and administrators, paid off the local police and military commanders to intimidate leftist and social-democratic groups active in the area, and has created a docile company union while destroying the independent labor groups. Some argue that La Romana has thus become a "company town," that the company has inordinate control over all aspects of the city's and region's life. Others respond that La Romana is thriving and that Gulf and Western has brought jobs and prosperity. Despite these disagreements, La Romana itself has continued to grow, and the recent completion of a huge new tourist complex further enhances its possibilities. La Romana has consequently become one of the most important medium-sized cities in the country; its future, however, is intimately tied up with the future of Gulf and Western.

Bonao

Bonao is another "boom town." Halfway between Santo Domingo and Santiago, Bonao has become the nation's mining center. With a population of just twenty-five thousand, Bonao is one of the smallest urban centers in the Dominican Republic. However, in the early 1970s rich deposits of nickel, bauxite, silver, and gold were found in the region. Foreign mining companies began their operations, and Bonao was transformed almost literally overnight from a sleepy, dusty crossroads to a boom area. Bonao faced an immediate influx of foreign engineers and executives, native construction workers, and thousands of unskilled Dominicans seeking work in the mines.

Today Bonao reflects the vast changes taking place in the Dominican Republic. With the desire to diversify the economy and lessen the traditional dependence on sugar, the national government is increasing its involvement in the mining of precious metals. The commitment to mining has made Bonao one of the most talked-about cities in the country. In its public relations efforts the government constantly refers to three achievements: the restoration of old Santo Domingo, the tourist developments on the northern coast, and the importance of the Bonao mining region.

As with any boom town, and parallel to the situation in La Romana, the sudden influx of new people, especially foreigners, and of new money, has created major tensions. A key problem in Bonao is the sharp separation in the city between the foreign enclave with its American-style ranch houses and way of life, and the shanties and poverty of the Dominicans. Some Dominicans have benefited from the boom, but many have been forced to work in the mines for pitifully low wages and in dangerous conditions. The greater use of automated techniques has also made these workers increasingly expendable. But as in La Romana, the tensions, social problems, and potential conflicts lying just below the surface have been submerged – for now – by prosperity and new money.

THE DOMINICAN PEOPLE AND THEIR CULTURE

To describe the Dominican Republic only in terms of its geography, landscape, resources, and demography, is to ignore some essential ingredients. As with any country, it is the people – their social and racial patterns, their ethnic heritage, their religious beliefs, language patterns, personality profile and behaviors – in short, their culture – that forms the foundation for national identity.

Unlike many of the Latin American nations, the Dominican Republic is relatively homogeneous in terms of its racial composition. The native Indian population was quickly decimated by conquest, forced labor, and the diseases carried by the Spaniards for which the Indians had no immunity. Within fifty years of the Spanish colonization, the native population and culture had been almost completely eliminated.

The Spaniards brought in African labor to replace the Indians in the mines and plantations. Over time a complex racial "melting pot" was formed, in which the mulatto became the dominant element numerically. Today nearly two-thirds of the Dominican population is officially listed as mulatto. Within that category, numerous subtle shadings and subcategories are used by the Dominicans.

Although the mulatto is most numerous, the country has historically been led by its white, Hispanic elements. Whites dominate business, finance, the prestigious professions, government, and high society. Mulatto elements are preponderant in the military officer corps, the provincial towns, the less prestigious professions, and among lower- to middle-level government officials.

Race and class are closely tied together. The white element tends to be wealthier and to form the Dominican elite. The middle classes tend to be mulatto. The working classes, rural and urban, tend to be black or dark mulatto. Despite the claims of some Dominicans to the contrary, racism is present in the Dominican Republic and there is no doubt that as one moves up the social scale, race is a very important factor separating social classes and economic positions. In comparison with the United States there is relatively little manifest racial prejudice in the Dominican Republic, seldom an expression of racial hatred among Dominican nationals, and little segregation along strictly racial lines. But recent incidents of racial violence between Dominicans and Haitians who have

Dominican children

settled in the country have forced many to reevaluate the whole issue of race relations.

In addition to these dominant racial categories, there are small pockets of other ethnic and nationality groups in the Dominican Republic. The important business and financial community of Santo Domingo contains a considerable number of Lebanese members. Many of the finest restaurants in the capital are owned by Chinese. A number of Italian and French families have gained influence. A few Jewish families remain, of the hundred or so who came as refugees during the period of the Holocaust. There is a community of Japanese farmers and, of course, a large community of Americans. Many Haitians and West Indians, brought in during the cane-cutting season, have stayed within Dominican borders.

Although there is considerable diversity in the country's racial and ethnic makeup, language and religion are a different story. Because of the absence of a native Indian population and the dominance of the Spanish tradition, the Dominican Republic is almost exclusively a Spanish-speaking nation. There are some regional dialects, but Spanish is *the* language of the country. Moreover, Dominican Spanish is a very clear, almost classical Spanish, in keeping with the Dominicans' pride in being the first settled colony and having the "purest" Spanish traditions in Latin America.

The proximity to North America and the powerful influence of the United States in the Dominican Republic has led to some "coca-colaization" of the language and culture. Baseball is the national sport, and American music and styles are widespread. "Home-run" is almost the same whether rendered in English or Spanish.

The dominance of the Spanish language is matched by the centrality of the Catholic Church and Catholic beliefs and culture. Approximately 98 percent of the Dominican population is Catholic. As with many nations, this figure does not represent actual participation in Church sacraments, but it does reflect the centrality and pervasiveness of the country's Catholicism.

The Dominican Catholic Church prides itself on its strong historical roots dating back to Columbus and its defense of the hapless Indians, and on its contributions to Dominican culture and society. For a long time the Dominican hierarchy had a reputation for conservatism and unwillingness to become involved in matters of social justice and political repression. At two critical junctures in Dominican history, during the Trujillo dictatorship (1930–1961) and in the 1965 revolution, the Church was seen as playing an overly passive and conservative role while many Dominicans were suffering.

The Church nonetheless remains a strong and vital part of Dominican society. Its influence is major in the areas of education and health, as well as religion. On some political issues (family planning, divorce, even the choice of a president) the Church's voice can be powerful. The past prominence as well as present dilemmas of the Church were recognized by Pope John Paul II, who made the Dominican Republic the first stop on his Latin American tour. The Pope's visit both dramatized the Dominican Republic's status as a Catholic nation and pointed to the problems for the Church (lack of funds, priests, social programs, or much political clout) existent there.

The hardest task in describing a nation other than one's own is to define precisely its special character and culture without falling into the dangers of oversimplification and stereotyping. There are always exceptions, of course, and making generalizations about a country's unique or dominant behavior can be dangerous. We need to keep these limitations in mind, but it is useful also to try to understand those cultural patterns that appear constant in Dominican society.

As in many of the Latin American nations, one is initially struck in the Dominican Republic by the male dominance and the sense of *machismo* that males display. The outward concern to appear strong and domineering, the prideful prance when others are looking, the sexual comments to passing females, the camaraderie among males, and the double standard that applies in the relations of husbands, wives, and mistresses, are but a few of the manifestations of an underlying need to appear superior and in control, sexually and otherwise. Male children are coddled, spoiled, and not disciplined; certainly this early experience is reflected in their later social and political behavior.

Machismo also helps explain why power is in the hands of males while women are expected to be docile, protected, and submissive. More and more Dominican women are working, however, joining the professions, and playing an increasing role in politics (President Joaquín Balaguer named women to serve as governors of all the nation's provinces); the Dominican women's movement is still weak, but change is clearly in the air. Furthermore, evidence is accumulating that although the male is the strong partner outside the home, the woman is dominant within the home, managing the family and controlling the purse strings.

If the machismo of Dominican males is readily observable, so too is the friendliness and expressiveness of the people. Despite its history of misfortune, the Dominican Republic has a well-deserved reputation for goodwill and personal warmth. Dominicans are cordial in greeting, patient and expressive in conversation, and gracious in parting. On a larger scale Dominicans reveal a sense of joy and passion that makes for a society of street corner singing, fiercely dedicated baseball fans, and explosive political demonstrations.

Beneath these outward expressions of gaiety, friendliness, politeness, and passion, there is a noticeable strain of quiet resignation—but also perseverance. Surprisingly, the suffering that Dominicans have endured historically from both domestic tyrants and foreign oppressors has registered not so much in the form of anger or bitterness (although there are those who display such feelings), but more in terms of a fatalistic acceptance of their lot and a desire to return to normalcy. Dominicans have a clear vision of a better tomorrow but experience has led them to be reluctant to take risks to achieve their hopes. After centuries of neglect, backwardness, wars, repression, dictatorship, under-development, intervention, and hurricanes, such resignation should not be too surprising.

This history also lies at the heart of Dominican political attitudes, particularly the lingering influence of Trujillo and his system of dominance, authority, and control. Although Trujillo was assassinated in 1961, his memory, style, and system survive.

Although many Dominicans express outward hatred of Trujillo, they tend to admire him secretly for his strength, showmanship, and na-tional accomplishments. Trujillo and Trujilloism are constant topics of conversation in the Dominican Republic, for Trujillo was a *caudillo*, a man on horseback, a *macho* authority figure *par excellence*, and much of what can be described as sociopolitical analysis in the country still begins and almost literally ends with Trujillo. One's evaluation of the success or failure of virtually any regime in recent Dominican history almost always uses Trujillo as the measuring rod, for good or ill.

Dominicans seem to have a love-hate relationship with Trujillo. They hated his bloody terror, the stifling censorship, the torture and secret police. But they admire his economic accomplishments, his machismo, the attention he brought the country, the "show" he put on, his ability to impose order and organization on an unruly country. As one prominent Dominican said to the authors, "There is a little of Trujillo in all of us."

Trujillo has been gone now for some twenty years, but Dominicans continue to see his influence on the body politic. His heirs and followers are still active: Joaquín Balaguer, president from 1966 to 1978, clearly modeled his regime on that of Trujillo (but without the terror), and Tru-jillo's popularity remains strong, especially in times of national breakdown and chaos (which occur frequently in the Dominican Republic). The sense of order and discipline he provided, the economic development he helped usher in, and his personal involvement in the lives of his subjects, are all attractive to Dominicans—all the more so because those features have been so rare in Dominican history. Many have sought to suppress or repudiate the things that Trujillo stood for, but that is hard because these traits are so strongly Dominican and the Trujillo regime so much a reflection of Dominican society and values.

Trujilloism seems to be a system of values and institutions that Dominicans publicly disavow but privately cannot. Liberal democracy is also a recurring theme that many other Dominicans would like to see established but that they seem unwilling or unable to achieve. Dominican history is full of numerous but largely unsuccessful efforts to establish a democratic system. Thus, while Dominicans admire democracy in the abstract, they are often skeptical of whether it can work in their country, given its disorder and lack of organization, and they often secretly prefer the authority and unity of strong-man rule.

The repeated failures of democracy and democratic governments have not, however, curtailed the commitment of many Dominicans to achieve democracy and constitutionalism. Throughout its long history of dictatorial rule, the passion of Dominicans for democracy did not falter, but grew stronger. Some of the most influential democratic movements grew most rapidly during the periods of strongest authoritarian rule.

The passion for democracy so strongly present in Dominican politics exists alongside the desire for unified, disciplined, authoritarian rule. These two traditions, the one democratic and the other authoritarian, run parallel in the national history. The country is caught between these two conflicting visions. The Dominicans would like to have democracy but they are somewhat fearful of its consequences and uncomfortable with the disorder, the license, the potential for chaos that this implies. They also admire discipline and order, but they do not want the oppressive tyranny into which this all too often degenerates. So far they have not found a proper formula for blending or reconciling these opposing currents that run so strongly throughout their life as a nation.

We should mention, finally, the way Dominican political culture has been influenced by its multifaceted relationship with the United States. That too is a mix of love and hate. In few countries has the United States's presence been so strong or so persistent over such a long time. That presence has brought economic development and a measure of protection to the Dominicans, but it has also brought exploitation and unwarranted interference in internal Dominican affairs.

The American influence is political, military, economic, and cultural, and it affects all areas of Dominican life. Perhaps its most interesting effects can be seen in the attitudes of the Dominican people. Americans who visit the country often marvel at the kind reception they receive from the people. Outwardly most Dominicans express fondness for the United States and the American way of life; there is little manifest anti-Americanism.

These appearances, however, cannot mask the ambivalence many Dominicans feel, the suspicion and mistrust many of them have but are too polite to express. Most Dominicans are too pragmatic to be carried away by the rhetoric of the anti-Yankee hatemongers present in the country, but they know enough of past Dominican history to view American political leaders, corporate administrators, and embassy personnel with some apprehension. They are respectful and often cooperative, but they seek to keep their distance. Americans bring in tourist dollars, new technology, and foreign aid; but Dominicans know there is a price to be paid in terms of loss of sovereignty, dependence on the "colossus of the north," and the Americanization of their culture.

What is astounding is not this wariness, but that the history of repeated U.S. intervention and manipulation has not completely soured Dominican-U.S. relations. After all, it was not long ago (1965) that American troops had occupied the Dominican Republic and were shooting at Dominicans whom the Americans had erroneously assumed to be Castro-Communists. It is a testament to the patience, long-sufferingness, stoicism, and capacity of Dominicans to forgive that they have not become virulently anti-American, but rather have chosen to cooperate with a neighbor that historically has treated the country as if it were a satellite and not a sovereign nation.

The simple little island paradise that Columbus sighted in 1492 has since become a complex and diversified nation. Its aspirations include economic growth and independence, a fairer and more equitable distribution of income, political stability and democracy, a small but dignified place in the Caribbean sun. These are modest goals, but they have been thwarted repeatedly by domestic politics, internal social and class rigidities, and by the international contingencies over which the Dominicans have no control.

These forces have served to retard the nation's development, and coupled with an incredible and often bizarre history, a complex racial melting pot, some major distortions in the economy, and conflicting cultural traditions, they have left the Dominican Republic a country of contradictions. Unable to break with a past that is authoritarian, elitist, semifeudal; its destiny shaped as often by foreign conquests and intervention as by domestic needs; mired in enormous social and economic problems; and unable to devise a political formula for development that resolves its various contradictions, the Dominican Republic represents an uneasy joining together of tradition and modernity, conflict and stability, wealth and poverty, idealism and cynicism.

To some, these contradictions reinforce the notion that the Dominican Republic is just another Third World country struggling to overcome its past. To the Dominicans, however, these contradictions reveal the essence of their heritage and their challenge for the future—their desire to resolve or live with their problems on their own terms, and to devise a uniquely Dominican developmental formula rather than some pale and retarded imitation of the already developed nations. As we move forward and examine the course of Dominican history, its social and economic structure and relations, and the nature of its political system, it will be possible to assess to what extent the Dominican Republic will be able to deal successfully with these wrenching contradictions in its national life.

3

The Pattern of Historical Development

The course of Dominican history is intricate, often chaotic, sometimes regressive, consistently fascinating. It is not a history of gradual, evolutionary, and inevitable progress toward some agreed-upon goal or a national "manifest destiny." Rather, Dominican history consists of starts and stops, forward surges and throwbacks to earlier and simpler eras, great turmoil and ruinous foreign interventions, slow and gradual change that is then frustrated by domestic tyrants, natural disasters, and unfinished and frustrated revolutions. Throughout the course of this history some common themes appear and reappear, shaping this unique and often unfortunate legacy.

THE COLONIAL ERA

To properly understand Dominican history we must go back not just to its declaration of independence but to the colonial era, to the powerful legacy implanted by Spain on Hispaniola.

The discovery of the island by Columbus in 1492 was a major historical event, the beginning of a process by which European civilization was spread to the far-flung corners of the globe. Spain was the first great colonial power, and Latin America was the first of the non-Western areas to be drawn into the European orbit.

The Spanish decision to found Santo Domingo as its initial capital in the New World was at best a mixed blessing. For a time the colony flourished as a center of transplanted European culture. A walled enclave city grew up patterned after those of medieval Spain; churches were erected, schools and hospitals built, and commerce, agriculture, and mining flourished. But the native Indians were quickly decimated, black slavery was introduced, and a rigid two-class system, reinforced by racial criteria, was introduced.

The "civilizing" process undertaken by Spain was incomplete and short-lived. After the first fifty years, the more enterprising Spaniards moved on to other islands or to the mainland, where there was more gold and silver and more Indians to enslave. The Spaniards proved more interested in enriching themselves than in developing their New World colonies. The island of Hispaniola was an early victim of this exploitative, get-rich-quick philosophy. Once its native labor supply had been depleted and its readily available mineral wealth exhausted, it was quickly abandoned.

Although the *conquistadores* sailed off to Cuba, Mexico, and other territories, they left behind a powerful colonial legacy and a vision of a "golden age." The system of two-class social relations, of political authoritarianism and hierarchy, of a centralized and state-dominated economy and society, and of political and religious unity, had been strongly implanted on Hispaniola. Moreover, because these institutions were associated with the glory and prosperity of Hispaniola in its first fifty years, they continued to represent an ideal model to which subsequent Dominican regimes would aspire. The Spanish may have abandoned Santo Domingo, but they left their mark indelibly stamped on the society. In the establishment and remarkable perseverance of these institutions, the Dominican Republic can be viewed as both the first and the most typical Latin American state.

The diversion of colonial attention from Hispaniola to Mexico and elsewhere left the once proud and important outpost in a sad state of neglect. Hispaniola became an underpopulated, undeveloped, and forgotten colony that offered little to the mother country or even to passing pirates. Its once-flourishing mines and plantations were abandoned, the economy reverted to a more primitive subsistence state, and the city of Santo Domingo fell into a bedraggled condition. What trade existed was primarily in cowhides, for the staple commodities like sugar, cotton, and tobacco that would later make the economy grow again were not properly managed or developed. The island was socially, politically, and economically disorganized and unorganized.

For over two hundred years the colony remained in this depressed condition, hopelessly thrust into the back pages of the Spanish colonial empire. Weak and underdeveloped, no longer of interest to the Spanish crown, it eventually became, as the Caribbean itself became, an imperial frontier for the rivalries among that era's superpowers, a pawn to be bartered between them. In the late 1500s and throughout the seventeenth century, the French, Spanish, and British competed for control of the island. Dutch pirates also sought a foothold. Despite the opposition of the English, Spain ceded the western one-third of the island to the French in 1697. Nearly one hundred years later, although the Spanish part of the island had experienced a mild resurgence, the Madrid government was no longer able or willing to administer such a vast colonial empire. In 1795 the Spanish ceded the eastern two-thirds to France as well.

The contrasts between the French-controlled section of Hispaniola (by that time called Hayti) and the former Spanish colony were pronounced. By 1790 the French colony contained 520,000 people and, based on black slavery, was a prospering colony producing sugar and cotton. Indeed, among all the colonial possessions in the world at that time, Hayti was the most prosperous; at one time England gave serious thought to bartering its thirteen colonies in North America for Hayti!

On the other hand, in the larger Spanish-speaking territory on Hispaniola there were less than 100,000 people living on a meagre subsistence or from contraband trade in meat and hides with Hayti. Those who could afford to leave continued to abandon the colony for a better life elsewhere. What was left behind can only be described as the run-down remnant of Spanish administration and culture.

The granting of the eastern two-thirds of Hispaniola to France in 1795 brought no relief. In fact, the opposite occurred: the once-proud colony slid further downhill. The shift in control from Spain to France introduced a half century of repeated foreign intervention, maladministration, racial conflict, and ruination. The spark that ignited the blaze was the slave revolt in Hayti. Led by slave revolutionaries Toussaint L'Ouverture and Henry Dessalines, the rebels succeeded in establishing in Hayti (now spelled Haiti) the world's first black republic.

After defeating the French, the black armies moved eastward into the former Spanish colony. From 1804 to 1809 the Haitians, French, and Spanish fought to determine who would eventually control the entire island. The British, who had economic and imperial designs of their own, aided the Spanish in driving the Haitians back to the west. From 1809 to 1821, the eastern colony was restored to Spanish administration.

The vulnerability of the colony to the whims of colonial masters and expansionist neighbors was made clear once more in 1821. The Spanish had again bungled as colonial administrators; and the Dominicans had, along with the other Latin American territories, declared their independence. Within weeks, however, Haitian armies had again overrun the entire island. Under their military leader Jean Pierre Boyer, the Haitians swept across Hispaniola, leaving a trail of blood and destruction. This Haitian occupation, 1822–1844, is often viewed as the initial cause of the racial, social, and political antagonism that even today separates Dominicans from Haitians. However, there were also some positive elements in the occupation, particularly the freeing of the slaves.

The Dominicans continued to view the Haitians as interlopers more interested in plunder than effective administration, and soon sentiment for independence grew. The leader of the independence movement was a philosopher, visionary, and literary romantic named Juan Pablo Duarte. While most of Latin America's great liberators had since left the scene, Duarte had not forgotten their impassioned cries for democracy and independence. Duarte and his associates formed a secret society, "La Trinitaria," that led the independence movement.

THE INDEPENDENCE ERA

By 1844 the Haitian hold on the increasingly nationalistic Dominicans was waning. An earthquake that had struck in 1842, destroying numerous Dominican cities, helped catalyze the opposition. Haiti itself was torn by domestic rivalries and civil war. With financial backing from Venezuela, Duarte and his fellow conspirators attacked the Haitian garrisons in a surprise move that led to a largely bloodless revolt. In 1844 he entered Santo Domingo triumphant, and the Dominican Republic was declared an independent nation.

The father of Dominican independence, however, was reluctant to wield the levers of power. While Duarte procrastinated and was soon exiled, political power was consolidated in the hands of two self-appointed generals, Buenaventura Báez and Pedro Santana. These two men soon stepped into the vacuum left by Duarte. Santana marched on the capital and declared himself dictator.

The rise to power of Santana and his "partner" in national leadership, Báez, ushered in what historians call the "era of the dual caudillos." For the next forty-five years these two "men on horseback" dominated Dominican politics, ruling directly or through compliant puppets. Santana and Báez alternated in the presidency and used their positions to enrich themselves at the public expense.

Although outside of personal enrichment it is difficult to decipher the national objectives of these two dictators, both had a vague design to restore the country to its earlier order and greatness and to develop close ties with a foreign protector. Both sought, unsuccessfully, to restore the sixteenth-century colonial model, complete with the protection of a benevolent large power. Both feared the continuous invasions of a more populous Haiti, and they approached, in turn, England, France, Spain, and the United States to offer an alliance and concessions as a way of safeguarding the country from invasion. The protectorate idea and the concessions, however, also made the Dominican Republic a dependency—sometimes a virtual colony—of these larger powers.

The Dominican Republic managed to hold off the Haitians and keep the larger nations at arm's length for a time, but by 1861 the country was bankrupt as a result of corruption, maladministration, disastrous

Independence Park, with part of the ancient city wall, in Santo Domingo

trade policies, and the constant need to repel Haiti's thrusts. Santana, now president for the third time, announced that the country would be reincorporated as a Spanish colony. By midsummer 1861, Santo Domingo was full of Spanish soldiers, officials, and priests who reintroduced the Spanish monopoly system of trade and administration. By midfall the Dominicans had already organized a revolt against Spanish rule. The nationalistic revolt also served to discredit Santana, who died in disgrace in 1864. Báez, however, still had many years left at the center of national politics.

With Santana out of the picture and Spain unable to maintain its hold, the new independence movement led by Gregorio Luperón met with scant resistance. The departure of the Spanish in 1865 opened up a new era of hope for Dominicans seeking lasting independence and the restoration of democratic government. Unfortunately, as before, poor leadership, divisions among the elite, and foreign intrigue helped stymie these hopes.

In 1865, Báez was inaugurated president for the third time, but his ascension to power immediately precipitated a rebellion by General Luperón. Forced to leave after only five months in office, Báez remained "on call," confident that his successors would fail. He was right.

In the midst of this "revolving door" brand of politics, Báez returned to power again in 1866 and promptly set about trying to negotiate loans and lease arrangements with several foreign powers (Britain, France, the United States), which were designed to extricate the country from its mounting indebtedness. Like Santana, Báez sought a foreign protector, and even tried to convince the Grant administration of the wisdom of annexing the Dominican Republic to the United States. The move failed by only one vote when the Senate acted on the treaty. These efforts to sell the country to the highest bidder touched off renewed rebellion and toppled Báez from power for the fourth time.

The years 1874–1879 were again marked by hope and promise as a reform president, Ulises Espaillat, came to power on the heels of Báez's overthrow. He promised to administer the nation's finances honestly and to govern constitutionally. Espaillat was in the tradition of Duarte, long on ideals but weak on practical realities. He proved unable to manage the contentious forces in the nation and soon fell from power. Báez returned again.

The fifth presidency of Báez was his shortest. Rebellion against him broke out immediately and he fell in two months – but not before pilfering $300,000 from the treasury and fleeing to Puerto Rico. In his wake Báez left a country bankrupt, factionalized, still dependent on foreign powers, and without any training in democratic self-government. While many Latin American countries were by this time consolidating their leaderships and developing economic stability, the Dominican Republic was still picking up the pieces of a chaotic and depressed society and economy anxious for relief from caudillo rule.

The political and economic disruptions occasioned by nearly a hundred years of repeated international traumas, Haitian occupations, and ruinous caudilloism came to an abrupt halt with the coming to power in 1882 of a modernizing dictator, Ulises Heureaux. For the next seventeen years Heureaux ran a tightly knit regime, again patterned on the "glorious" sixteenth-century Spanish model, which combined vigorous economic modernization with stern autocratic techniques designed to ensure his own position at the apex of the Dominican pyramid. A believer in order and progress, Heureaux was the first Dominican leader since independence to direct his energies toward goals other than selling away the national patrimony, enriching himself exclusively, and presiding over national strife.

Under Heureaux roads were built, railways constructed, irrigation canals dug, and telephone and telegraph lines installed. Immigration increased and the population grew. The stability that was established encouraged Cuban and other planters to expand sugar production, a step that would have profound implications for the future of the economy. Heureaux kept the Haitians from invading and also survived several challenges to his rule launched from the rich Cibāo farm region.

Heureaux was successful in achieving political order and economic modernization, but to accomplish his goals he was forced to float disadvantageous bank loans and lease the timber-rich Samana Peninsula and its Bay (the best natural port in the Caribbean) to foreign interests. Heureaux managed for a time to pay off part of the loans to German, French, British, and American interests, but the debts also demonstrated the degree of dependency of the Dominican economy on foreign capital.

The successes Heureaux achieved in the economic sphere did not lead to a complementary liberalization in the political. Instead, as time wore on he became more autocratic and corrupt. Hired assassins, corrupt sycophants, and networks of spies consisting of the president's mistresses were part of Heureaux's retinue and system of rule. Heureaux was a dictator who would court no opposition and did not hesitate to use brutal measures to ensure his unchallenged personal authority.

As Heureaux became more repressive, the opposition mounted. The fact that the president was black further diminished his stature among the white patricians of the Cibāo. The Heureaux era came to an end when one of the opposition leaders, Ramón Cáceres, walked up to Heureaux at a crowded public gathering and shot him. The death of Heureaux ended the Dominican Republic's first experiment with a modernizing dictatorship. It would not be the last time a Dominican leader would conclude that national development was only achievable by means of tight control, fear, and a complete dictatorial system.

Heureaux's assassination left another vacuum in Dominican politics that could not be filled by those who had plotted against him. Between 1899 and 1906, the country saw a return of the political factionalism, personal rivalries, and constant infighting that had gone before. The two most prominent leaders were Juan Isidro Jiménez and Horacio Vásquez. Vásquez had been the chief driving force in the anti-Heureaux movement, but he proved a weak and timid leader. Jiménez was a wealthy Cibāo landowner who seemed more interested in using the presidency to enrich himself further than in governing effectively.

By 1902 Dominican politics had again become a tinderbox as "Horacista" forces battled "Jimenistas." There were few ideological or programmatic differences between these two factions, but both leaders and their retinues wished to capture the National Palace – and the jobs and treasury that went with it. The conflict between these two factions not only created great instability, but also left the economy in shambles. The country's export trade was disrupted, foreign loans were not being paid, and foreign creditors were encouraging their governments to use gunboats to collect unpaid debts.

The near-bankruptcy of the Dominican Republic brought on by

political instability and disastrous foreign loans, and the threat of foreign powers to use force to collect, were the immediate causes of President Theodore Roosevelt's proclamation of his famous "Corollary" to the Monroe Doctrine. U.S. economic and strategic interests in the Dominican Republic had been increasing for some time; the country's present economic difficulties now meshed neatly with the expansionist designs of Roosevelt. At a time when the United States had acquired major interests in the Caribbean (Cuba, Puerto Rico, the Panama Canal) and was determined to play a leadership role throughout the hemisphere, the Dominican Republic's financial problems provided the United States with an opportunity to control the future of its poor, unstable neighbor. Shrewdly sensing how Dominican indebtedness could enhance U.S. influence, Roosevelt negotiated an agreement with interim President Carlos Morales under which 45 percent of the export revenues collected at Dominican customs houses (the principal source of government funds) would be delivered to the Dominican government for current expenses, while the remaining 55 percent would be administered by the United States to pay off the debts.

The receivership agreement between the United States and the Dominican Republic was ratified by both countries in 1907 (the Dominicans had little choice but to go along) and immediately helped extricate the Dominican Republic from its debt of about $295 million. It also increased enormously the U.S. presence (internal revenue agents, administrators, tax experts *plus* some troops to guard the agents) in the Dominican Republic.

In the meantime, Ramón Cáceres, the assassin of Heureaux, had ascended to the presidency, bringing five years of peace to a country badly in need of tranquility. With the economy and government receipts under the watchful eye of the United States, Cáceres brought political stability, some economic modernization, and much-needed efficient administration. He extended the road system, reformed local government, restructured public enterprises, and brought a level of professionalism to the armed forces. His successes, however, did not fundamentally alter Dominican political habits.

The Jimenista-Horacista conflict continued. Cáceres, while riding in his carriage in Santo Domingo, was assassinated by a Jimenista. The assassin of Heureaux had met his death at the hands of an assassin. Old wounds are not forgotten in the Dominican Republic, and even today the families involved remain bitter rivals and do not speak to each other. The two dominant figures of turn-of-the-century politics in the Dominican Republic, one an authoritarian modernizer and the other a democratic modernizer, were both slain, victims of the violence, jealousy, and personal rivalries that mark so much of Dominican history.

The death of Cáceres initiated another round of domestic political warfare, economic disruption, and, eventually, foreign occupation. By 1912, the Dominican government was violating the terms of the customs agreement and was slipping again into debt and political chaos. At the same time, the United States shifted its interest in Dominican affairs from economic concerns to political and strategic ones.

By 1916, with the Dominican political situation degenerating, World War I under way, and German influence spreading to Haiti, the Wilson administration began to recognize the need to secure Dominican stability through a military presence. On May 16 of that year Dominican President Jiménez had been impeached by the Dominican Congress, an action that set off a new wave of rebellion. The reaction of the United States was immediate. The *U.S.S. Dolphin* arrived at the northern coast and began unloading troops. Initially the U.S. forces did not claim control of the country, but sought the more limited goals of restoring order and the 1905 agreement. By November, as it became obvious the Dominicans would not knuckle under to American demands, the U.S. forces already present were authorized to proclaim military rule.

The U.S. occupation lasted eight years. These were years of economic growth, some modernization, and enforced political stability. The U.S. military fostered numerous public works projects (roads, telephones, port facilities), the foreign debt was decreased, educational facilities were built, and public health was improved. It is important to stress, however, that the United States was not so much an "enlightened civilizer" as a "pragmatic occupier." Its "modernization" of the Dominican Republic's land titles system allowed American sugar firms to expand their holdings, the new roads were designed to facilitate the mobility of the occupation military forces, and the public works projects were paid for with *Dominican* pesos.

The presence of the United States generated considerable opposition. Especially in the east (the sugar areas), bands of patriots (the Americans called them bandits) rose up in armed resistance. The records show the U.S. forces retaliated strongly against the rebels, which may help explain the especially strong anti-Americanism in this area even now. But is must also be said that unlike Nicaragua, where a guerrilla leader named Augusto Sandino rose to prominence and served as an inspiration for future generations, in the Dominican Republic the guerrilla resistance remained limited and no single charismatic leader emerged. In fact, given the earlier chaos, many Dominicans welcomed the occupation and profited from it.

By 1921, with World War I ended and a new administration in Washington, the United States had lost interest in its Dominican venture. During the next three years U.S. officials and Dominican leaders worked on a plan that would enable the United States to withdraw militarily while, it was hoped, maintaining political stability and economic solvency. The agent of stability was to be a new national military force, the *guardia*, trained and equipped by the U.S. Marines. New elections were held in 1924, and aging General Vásquez, leader of the old Horacista faction, was elected president. Two months later the U.S. flag was replaced by the Dominican tricolor, and that same year the Marines also left.

The U.S. occupation forces left behind them a nation somewhat more prosperous and urbanized than before, that had learned the joys of chewing gum and baseball, but not a nation that had overcome its past, forgotten old scores, or was equipped for democratic government. The Marines also left behind a national guard that would henceforth be the final arbiters of Dominican national politics, and a young, street-wise lieutenant named Rafael Trujillo, who would use the guard to seize and hold power, rule longer and more brutally than anyone previously in Dominican history, and become Latin America's most totalitarian dictator.

THE TRUJILLO ERA

The six years following the departure of the U.S. forces were stable and peaceful. Vásquez provided a needed respite from the heretofore constant turmoil. The tranquility proved to be only temporary, however, as the nation soon reverted to earlier trends. Rival groups challenged the president and began to plot his overthrow. They accused him of being a puppet of the United States. The president's health failed. The world depression of 1929–1930 ruined the nation's economy. The national guard, left behind by the U.S. Marines and now under the firm control of Trujillo, was a potential destabilizing force. With the country's arsenal in the hands of a highly trained military unit under ambitious leadership, political leaders without a firm base of support would need to be ever vigilant to the threat of a coup.

The fragility of democracy in the Dominican Republic was revealed in 1930 when a revolution was launched from Santiago against the Vásquez government. Rather than defending the government, the clever and ruthless head of the guard instead gave arms to the rebels and assured them he would not block their advance. A one-time telegraph operator and sugar plantation guard, Trujillo had risen rapidly through the ranks of the guardia by faithfully serving the Marines. Tough, ambitious, wanting wealth and social position, Trujillo prepared for the day when he could move out of the barracks and into the National Palace.

After Vásquez had been toppled, Trujillo convinced the rebels to lay down their arms. He encouraged the rebel leader, Rafael Estrella

Ureña, to run for president. But soon Trujillo was using strong-arm tactics to promote his own candidacy. He now "convinced" Estrella Ureña to run for the vice presidency. Other potential Trujillo opponents disappeared or were found slain, Trujillo's military henchmen used intimidation tactics on the citizenry, and the electoral machinery was taken over by Trujillo. Trujillo won the 1930 presidential election with more votes than there were eligible voters.

Trujillo's rise to power in 1930 was the result of ad hoc intimidation, manipulation, and fraud. His rule as president and dictator for the next thirty-one years saw the institutionalization of these features and the addition of others; namely, personal aggrandizement, economic control, and brutal and systematic repression. Trujillo would become the most important figure in Dominican history, a leader who presided over a period of tremendous importance in the nation's development and whose mode of operations and policy judgments would touch every aspect of Dominican life. In a real sense the Dominican Republic became an extension of the dictator, his personal "fiefdom." From 1930 to 1961 he completely dominated the country, holding all power and directly shaping virtually all of its daily activities. Even today, as we have seen, the Trujillo regime remains the most controversial topic in the Dominican Republic, defining its political spectrum, eliciting incredibly conflicting reactions, and largely determining the political views of the population.

Trujillo came to power as a usurper and authoritarian, and the conditions prevailing in 1930 served further the aggrandizement of his power. In September of that year the most destructive hurricane ever to hit the country leveled Santo Domingo and caused untold damage, injury, and loss of life. Trujillo used the tragedy to consolidate additional authority in his own hands and to rule by decree-law, without constitutional limitations. The depressed economic conditions caused by the market crash of 1929–1930 also enabled him to gather most of the financial reins in his own hands, to move from a system of private capitalism toward one in which the state (Trujillo himself) was the dominant influence, and to subordinate the major economic groups (business, labor, agriculture) to state (his own) direction.

The manner in which he attacked these early problems demonstrated clearly how he would tackle others later. He argued that the country's major difficulties were economic recovery and growth, and that it was impossible to talk about freedom and democracy in a country without roads, bridges, docks, agriculture, and so forth. He thus dispensed with all political freedoms.

Trujillo's formula for resolving the nation's economic problems was simple, direct, and not revolutionary. First, recovery and financial solvency rested on greater economic ties to the United States. To achieve this he granted the United States vast concessions and power over the Dominican economy – until he later became something of an economic nationalist. Second, he said, economic modernization could not be achieved without major sacrifices from the Dominican people. To that end he crushed all independent trade unions and squeezed the population dry to acquire capital for development and his own enrichment. Third, those who openly disagreed with his programs were subject to the vast repressive apparatus of the state. With this formula Trujillo went about the business of moving the Dominican Republic forward while also benefiting himself, his family, and his friends.

In the course of his long administration, Trujillo was responsible for a vast number of building projects and new economic enterprises. This, plus the peace and order of his regime in a country where economic growth and stable politics had been all but completely unknown, account for the popularity of his regime – then and now. The Dominican economy, under his strong hand and with favorable sugar prices, expanded at impressive rates.

As the economy flourished, so did Trujillo. Estimates of his wealth ranged from $300 million to about $1 billion. But the monetary figure for his personal wealth may be less important than the extent of his control over the entire national economy. Trujillo or his family members and friends had control of nearly 60 percent of the country's economic assets and about the same percentage of its labor force. They owned the best lands, the majority of the all-important sugar industry, the cement works, airlines, shipping concerns, tobacco fields, and dozens of other enterprises. In addition, most of the gainfully employed population worked for Trujillo, directly in his enterprises or indirectly as government employees.

Trujillo was a realist, which in his times and his part of the world dictated close ties to the United States. He posed as the Hemisphere's "Foremost Anti-Communist" and carefully cultivated favor in the United States. Trujillo tied his administration to the United States with trade, aid, and defense packages that had the important side effect of further bolstering his rule. During the Trujillo years the Dominican Republic received preferential treatment from the United States. Trujillo made sure the U.S.-Dominican Republic "pipeline" continued flowing by courting the support of presidents and key members of Congress.

What the United States chose to ignore (but which could not be ignored in the Dominican Republic) was the insidious terror and torture Trujillo used to consolidate and maintain his rule. Trujillo turned the Dominican Republic into a vast police state where obedience was a requirement of citizenship and opposition was met with swift and ruthless action.

Trujillo's terror even reached outside the Dominican Republic, as his agents sought out and executed leading opponents of his rule. Trujillo once went so far as to order the assassination of President Rómulo Betancourt of Venezuela, but the attempt narrowly failed. For his excesses Trujillo was condemned both by his own people and by world opinion.

Trujillo ran one of the tightest dictatorships the world had ever seen. The web of controls included military might, political and governmental absolutism, economic monopoly, thought control, educational and intellectual conformity, systematic terror, and control over all socioeconomic groups. But as with any regime that employs such totalitarian excesses, Trujillo and Trujilloism were bound eventually to self-destruct.

In the late 1950s, after thirty years of dominance and seemingly at the height of his power, Trujillo's regime began to break down. Sugar prices, the main source of foreign revenue, plummeted and undermined the economic strength of the country. The assassination attempt against Betancourt resulted in a trade and arms embargo against the Dominican Republic. The United States withdrew its support. Dominican society in the 1950s was also quite different from that of the 1920s. An urban labor force had grown up and a new middle class had emerged; they were impatient with Trujillo's excesses and monopolistic practices and eager both to liberalize Dominican society and to get a share of the wealth and power for themselves. The domestic opposition grew rapidly.

On May 30, 1961, Trujillo was assassinated along a stretch of highway just west of Santo Domingo while en route to visit his latest mistress. The seven-man assassination team did not represent the most oppressed sector of Dominican society, nor was the assassination accompanied by social revolution. Rather, the group came from the upwardly mobile middle class, from elements once close to the regime, who either had personal and family scores to settle or else saw Trujillo as an impediment to their own efforts to gain power and privilege. Though they succeeded in assassinating Trujillo, their plot to seize power failed; all but two of the assassins were subsequently rounded up and killed. The United States government was closely involved in the assassination.

The death of Trujillo brought to a close an important chapter in Dominican history and left an indelible mark on the national psyche. As with any political leader who rules for such an extended period of time, Trujillo remains the subject of endless analyses, interpretations, and reinterpretations. Recent examinations of the Trujillo era point to the developmental accomplishments of the dictator, his administrative and organizational talents, and his continuing popularity among many Dominicans who see him as having provided prosperity, normalcy, stability, and a measure of national prestige and power.

But to many others Trujillo will be remembered as a self-serving and bloody tyrant. His megalomania, torture chambers, corruption, and totalitarianism constitute their lasting picture of Trujillo's regime. Whatever one's final perspective of Trujillo, national savior or national destroyer or some combination of these, the dictator directed the course of Dominican history for over thirty years; the country and its institutions were all tremendously influenced by his rule. With his death, Dominican society experienced a massive collapse of leadership and a political and institutional vacuum. Few Dominicans remembered anything except life under Trujillo. With him gone the country had to redefine its identity and chart a new course, and it had neither the leadership, the institutions, nor the guideposts to do that.

4

Contemporary Dominican History

Trujillo's death ushered in one of the Dominican Republic's most turbulent eras. No longer was there a single leader who could hold the country together. And because so much power – military, governmental, economic – had been concentrated in Trujillo's hands, the country also lacked a core of middle-level officials who might have stepped into the void. The institutions to preserve continuity were wholly lacking. A variety of elites, old rich and new rich, long deprived of access to power and wealth by the dictator's monopoly, now vied to recapture the National Palace and the funds and positions that went with it. Exile groups returned and new political parties and labor unions were formed. This was also the time of Castro's coming to power and of strong efforts by the United States to prevent "another Cuba" in the neighboring Dominican Republic. The Dominican cauldron soon began to boil.

AFTER TRUJILLO

The months immediately after the assassination were chaotic, but the power structure did not change. The news of Trujillo's death did not bring a national outpouring of joy – the Dominican people did not pour into the streets in victory parades. Instead, the streets remained quiet, filled only with military and secret police units rounding up and sometimes executing – right on the sidewalks – anyone thought to have had a hand in the assassination. The dictator was gone but the Trujillo system remained intact for the time being.

Power had been inherited by Ramfis Trujillo, the dictator's son, and by Joaquín Balaguer, one of a number of puppet presidents through whom the old tyrant had ruled. They tried to maintain the regime and go about business as usual, but it soon became clear they could not hope to wield the power or exert the authority that Trujillo had for thirty-one years. Domestic opposition mounted. The United States also put pressure on them to democratize. Anxious to push democratic re-formism, and fearful that another Castro would seize power if it did not, the United States advised Ramfis and Balaguer that future good relations between the two countries depended on signs of progress toward democracy.

The Dominican leaders felt the pressure and saw the handwriting on the wall. Within weeks Balaguer was allowing exiles to return and permitting opposition parties to form. Political activity resumed for the first time in over three decades. Three major groups emerged. The National Civic Union (UCN), which represented the business community and was led by Viriato Fiallo, organized a series of demonstrations and general strikes against Balaguer and Ramfis aimed at getting rid of the Trujillo influence. It constituted the strongest early opposition to the regime. Potentially more important than the UCN was the Dominican Revolutionary Party (PRD), a social-democratic party founded by Juan Bosch in exile and now allowed to return to lay the groundwork for a popular movement based on social reform. The third group was the Fourteenth of June Movement, whose followers included many students and young people and which came eventually to represent the pro-Castro element.

The pressures from these groups, in concert with Dominican labor and professional associations, further increased the dilemmas for Ramfis and Balaguer. They wanted to maintain the Trujillo system and their own positions on the one hand, but on the other they faced almost daily criticism and pressure from the United States and from their own people, who sensed their weakness.

In November 1961, unable to stem the unrest and not very adept at politics, Ramfis and the rest of the Trujillo family fled the country – but not without first emptying the treasury of $90 million. Balaguer re-mained behind, but was forced to share power in a seven-man Council of State that included businessmen, clergy, politicians from the UCN, and the two surviving Trujillo assassins. Inaugurated on January 1, 1962, the Council of State pledged to hold elections before the end of the year.

But stability and democracy were not yet assured. Two weeks after the Council's inauguration, a military coup occurred. Two days later another coup reversed the first one and restored the Council of State, but this time without Balaguer, who was forced to leave the country. Balaguer left, however, not as a hated figure like Ramfis, but with con-siderable respect. He had helped instigate a cautious democratization, he was not identified with the bloody reprisals of the Trujillos, and he had built a following by vast giveaways of the past dictator's properties. His performance would stand him in good stead later, both among the Dominican people longing for a return to authoritarian normalcy, and among U.S. officials looking for a popular but conservative leader. The second Council of State, now supported by most military units and strongly aided by the United States, sought to preserve order while also providing for gradual democratization. Again made up of conservatives and businessmen, and led by lawyer Rafael Bonnelly, the Council survived but did not flourish. It was under great pressure to move quickly toward democracy, but because of the social and class makeup of its members it was often reluctant.

The Council achieved some notable successes: It provided freedom and a measure of reconstruction, and it carried out the scheduled elections. But the problems were immense. Most Dominicans knew nothing of democracy or what it meant. Funds were scarce and the national administration, after so many years under Trujillo, was a shambles. Conservative elites were highly apprehensive about the prospect of democracy and they proved reluctant to cooperate and ready to find fault. The military, fearing its privileges would be taken away, was restless.

DEMOCRACY AND REVOLUTION

As the parties organized and prepared for December elections, it became increasingly clear that the PRD had the largest popular following. For years it had been the most active exile opposition group. The party had by now built a strong grass-roots organization in all areas of the country. Its program of social reform under democratic auspices was attractive. And in Juan Bosch it had an articulate, fiery, charismatic leader.

The election outcome was therefore no surprise. Bosch and the PRD defeated Fiallo and the UCN by a 2-1 margin. The PRD's stunning victory represented the triumph of the urban and rural masses over the country's traditional ruling elites in the upper and upper-middle classes.

The victory also meant an enormous challenge for the new president and his party. Elected on a platform of economic reform and social justice, the new government needed to deliver on its promises to the masses, but at the same time it had to recognize constraints and deal realistically with powerful conservative and vested interests: the Church, the military, the economic plutocracy, and the U.S. embassy.

At first the Bosch government moved energetically to keep its promise of democratic social revolution. But as the weeks and months passed, it became evident that such extensive changes could not so easily be attained. Some blamed the intransigence of the elite groups, others felt the PRD government was ill-equipped to administer the government, still others saw Juan Bosch as a hapless romantic who could not translate ideology into action. Whatever the reason, the reforms promised by

Bosch and the PRD never got off the ground.

Despite the government's lackluster performance, it nevertheless received the concerted opposition of the country's historic ruling groups. The opposition was based more on the potential threat these interests felt than on anything the government actually did. Soon the Church was opposed, the Army was rumbling, the economic elites were protesting, and the U.S. embassy became disenchanted. That coalition is enough to topple any Dominican government.

The issue that united them all was anticommunism. Bosch had promised to allow a climate of freedom, including freedom for Marxist groups. That enraged the stand-pat elements, who were convinced the country was about to become another Cuba. They declared the government was infiltrated by Communists. Although the charges were wildly inaccurate and though the Dominican Communist groups were woefully weak and disorganized, the reliability of the accusations became secondary to the effect they had of unifying the opposition and undermining the government.

The military, led by Colonel Elías Wessin y Wessin (soon promoted to general), staged a coup in September 1963, overthrowing the Bosch government after only seven months in office. The coup was bloodless and did not stimulate a widespread progovernment response among its earlier supporters.

With Bosch forced into exile in Puerto Rico, the military established a three-man civilian *junta* soon dominated by Santo Domingo businessman Donald Reid Cabral. But Reid Cabral was not a popular or strong leader. He was viewed as an antidemocratic interloper and as a front for the military. Corruption and repression increased.

The unpopularity and weakness of the government stimulated a renewal of plotting and intrigue – again that familiar pattern. A variety of groups opposed Reid Cabral but often for diverse reasons. Some were interested purely in wealth and personal power. Convinced that the president would never hold the free elections once promised, some PRD activists began a plot to restore Bosch and constitutional government by staging a coup themselves. Leftist students and others planned a Castroite revolution. Businessmen wanted a more honest government that listened closely to them. Rival military factions jockeyed for power, and former president Balaguer was scheming to make a comeback.

On April 24, 1965, the PRD moved to seize power. The revolution was led by both the old PRD civilians and a new group of younger military officers. The rebels struck quickly, taking over key positions in Santo Domingo. PRD leader Juan Francisco Peña Gómez went on radio to alert the people to the revolution. The announcement sent thousands of people into the streets. Rebel or "Constitutionalist" troops occupied the presidential palace. In Puerto Rico an ecstatic Bosch made plans to return. José Molina Ureña, formerly head of the Chamber of Deputies under Bosch and thus constitutionally the next in line for the presidency, was sworn in on an interim basis.

But the PRD takeover of the Palace and Reid Cabral's fall did not elicit unanimous rejoicing, especially from conservative and military interests or the U.S. embassy. For a short time the conservatives seemed paralyzed, unable to respond. Meanwhile, as the rebellion spread, Dominicans celebrated Reid Cabral's overthrow and the restoration of constitutionalism.

The celebration was premature. On April 26, encouraged by the United States, General Wessin and the military launched a counterattack. Air Force jets strafed the National Palace and rebel strongholds throughout the city. Heavy fighting took place at the Duarte Bridge, the major entry point into the city from the east, where weakly armed civilians repelled the efforts of the military tanks to cross and crush the rebellion.

The early fighting inflicted great loss on the constitutionalists who could not control the skies and were often cut down by the tanks. They could not convince the military commanders to surrender, nor were they successful in spreading the revolution to the rest of the country. Yet they persevered, and in a decisive battle on April 28, the popular forces drove the military back and seemed on the verge of defeating it.

Although the chief combatants in this civil war were the pro-Bosch constitutionalists against the conservative military, the deciding factor was the United States. Early in the rebellion the embassy had made a decision that it did not want Bosch back. Ambassador Tapley Bennett soon began reporting to Washington on the supposed communist infiltration of the constitutionalist forces. As the conflict went on it became obvious that the United States was not interested in a cease-fire or a negotiated settlement, but favored a victory by loyalist forces to prevent the possibility of "another Cuba."

This initial embassy strategy backfired. Rather than crushing the rebels, the Dominican military disintegrated and seemed poised on the brink of defeat. Rebel military leaders Francisco Caamaño and Manuel Montes Arache took over the constitutionalists' leadership and rallied their forces. In some of the fiercest fighting of the war, they pushed the regular military out of the city.

Seeing the military it had counted on to defeat the rebels and restore order about to go under, the United States intervened. On April 28, under President Johnson's orders, U.S. military forces were flown into the capital city, ostensibly to protect and evacuate American citizens, but in reality to halt the constitutionalist advance.

The buildup of U.S. forces (eventually 23,000 troops) opened a new chapter in the civil war. The U.S. troops surrounded the constitutionalists and ultimately, as in 1916–1924, occupied the entire country. The intervention brought home to Dominicans – and Latin Americans – the extent to which the United States would go to prevent a possible "second Cuba" in the Caribbean. The United States was paranoid with this "second Cuba" complex, intervening in the Dominican case even where no credible communist threat existed.

It is important to stress at this point that though there were communist and *Fidelista* elements in the revolution, they were by no means the dominant elements. It was a gross exaggeration on the part of the United States to describe the revolution as communist inspired or led. The rebellion was an intricate and multifaceted movement made up of several currents. The two most important elements, the PRD civilians and the constitutionalist military, were anything but communist. Their program was a return to constitutional government not unlike that of the United States.

The realities and complexities of the civil war, however, did not interest Johnson or his advisers. What concerned them was the prevention at all costs of a second Cuba. Johnson reasoned that no American president could be reelected if he permitted a second Cuba in the Caribbean; also, in 1965 he was in the midst of preparing for the massive buildup of U.S. forces in Viet Nam. His intervention in Santo Domingo was meant to send a message to the North Vietnamese of U.S. strength and a willingness to use it.

Seeking to stabilize the Dominican Republic meant neutralizing the constitutionalists while giving the loyalists a chance to regroup and rearm. To achieve this goal the U.S. troops established a corridor between the opposing forces. American forces then swept through the city or used the Dominican army to crush the constitutionalists, except in their stronghold in the old city.

Although the Americans stopped short of completely eliminating the constitutionalists, their revolution was aborted. Meanwhile, the United States sought to put a more favorable face on its military intervention by "internationalizing" the peace-keeping forces with small contingents of troops from other countries. The creation of the Inter-American Peace Force (IAPF), hastily assembled under American pressure by the Organization of American States (OAS), did little to alter the realities of the situation. The IAPF was always viewed by Dominicans and Latin Americans alike as purely an American creation. U.S. military commanders remained in control. Except for the Costa Ricans, all the troops came from countries governed by rightist dictatorships.

The U.S. intervention stimulated intense anti-Americanism. But the United States, once its initial objective of preventing the revolution from succeeding had been achieved, worked tirelessly to extricate itself from the imbroglio. After months of negotiation and on-again, off-again fighting, Col. Caamaño, the constitutionalist leader, and General Imbert, who led conservative forces, arranged a cease-fire. The war was brought to a close on August 31, 1965, when both parties, under U.S. pressure, signed an Institutional Act and an Act of Reconciliation. The agreements called for the naming of a provisional president and the holding of new elections. Héctor García-Godoy, a moderate Santiago oligarch, became interim president, achieved a modicum of order, and called new elections for June 1, 1966.

Before moving on, it is important to reflect on the 1965 crisis. Much has been written about the revolution and intervention, most of it from an American perspective. Some critics fault the U.S. embassy and its uninformed reporting. Other analysts wonder about the capacity of the United States to deal with profound social and political change in the Third World without falling prey to cold war dogmas and anticommunist phobias. Still others view the crisis in terms of the larger crisis of the Viet Nam war and the emerging role of the United States as policeman of the world. There are even a few ideologues who, ignoring all the evidence and accepting the falsifications put out by the U.S. government, actually laud the intervention.

Amidst these conflicting interpretations, little attention has been devoted to the meaning of the crisis for the Dominican people and nation. Approximately two thousand Dominicans were killed in the revolution or as a result of the intervention; thousands of others suffered injuries, some permanent. But the social and psychological scars may be just as important. In the revolution, a weak and struggling people and nation had seen their hopes raised, then dashed as the Americans intervened. A society that had suffered so much in the past but had persevered and sought a better day was again crushed, spiritually as well as physically.

The revolution of 1965 was not so much about communism as it was about democracy and the Dominicans' ability to manage their own destiny. To the Dominicans, the revolution involved their basic drives as a nation: self-determination, dignity, sovereignty, national pride, that modest place in the sun for which they had always hoped. "In a deeper sense," writes Piero Gleijeses, "the Dominican crisis began with the arrival of Christopher Columbus at the fair island of Hispaniola." Since the days of Columbus the Dominicans have had to live not only with underdevelopment, but also with the fact of their own weakness and susceptibility to foreign intervention. In 1965 the Dominicans had a chance to overcome their dependency, but instead they were reminded again of their subservience. It was a hard lesson to master, and also one that is indelibly marked on the soul of all Dominicans. They will not forget.

THE UNFINISHED REVOLUTION

The Dominican Republic's revolution was an unfinished revolution. The American intervention solved none of the underlying problems – poverty, inequality, and the like – that had caused the revolution; it merely postponed the reckoning. The simmering cauldron that is the Dominican Republic is almost certain to boil over again.

The revolution and intervention had a profound effect on all Dominicans, but it also, we are convinced, had a profound effect on the United States. The United States was caught in a web of lies, its Latin America policy was totally discredited, and the credibility of the government and President Johnson was undermined. The Dominican intervention was probably the first major event leading to the crisis of confidence in the U.S. government that would later reach crescendo proportions over Viet Nam and Watergate. One author has written, with a measure of exaggeration but with much truth as well, that the day the United States intervened in the Dominican Republic was the day the United States lost the cold war in the Third World. Hence, the intervention was not only a disaster for the Dominicans; in the long run it may have been a disaster for the United States as well.

The conclusion of a peace agreement between the contending Dominican factions, the naming of a moderate as provisional president, and the calling of new elections gave the Dominicans a "breather," but the scars remained deep. The fighting had brought widespread economic dislocations, intense political antagonisms, and much hatred and bitterness. Although President García-Godoy sought to provide an atmosphere for political and economic reconstruction, there was little possibility of uniting the country for a common development effort. Dominican society was hopelessly divided between the forces of the status quo, who in most respects emerged victorious as a result of the U.S. occupation, and the constitutionalists, who saw victory snatched from their grasp and a reimposition of the older system of corruption, authoritarianism, and special favoritism.

Given such divisions, it is not surprising that this era of supposedly "new beginnings" was hopelessly flawed and doomed to failure. The conservative elites now back in power and supported by the United States showed disdain for any opposition to their plan to have the venerable Trujillo puppet, Joaquín Balaguer, brought back and elected president.

The opposition PRD and their candidate Bosch, who was allowed to return from exile, were viewed as unacceptable electoral alternatives, especially among the military and police forces.

The United States also supported Balaguer. There had long been an admiration in the U.S. government for Balaguer, who, in contrast to Bosch, was seen as someone who could get things done. The Johnson administration, committed to the social reforms of the Great Society on the domestic front, felt that it could ill afford to gamble on a temperamental democrat like Bosch and felt more comfortable with the conservative Balaguer, even though he signalled a reinstitution of what was now being termed "neo-Trujilloism."

The tactics used to frustrate Bosch's campaign reminded Dominicans that the new ruling groups would not tolerate a fully democratic system. Bosch and his demoralized PRD supporters faced constant threats and recriminations from police and military forces. Some PRD leaders were subject to terroristic attacks that left them wounded or maimed; others were found dead, or they just disappeared. The climate of fear kept Bosch from leaving the capital city, while the systematic repression kept his aides and supporters prudently quiet.

Balaguer, with no fear of reprisals and his campaign lavishly supported by Dominican and foreign funds, moved easily and confidently about the country. He centered his campaign in the campo, where the revolution had not reached, and in the conservative Cibão, where most of the population still lived. Everywhere he went Balaguer used a low-key approach to instill a sense of confidence and to play down the idea that he was a new Trujillo. To all his audiences Balaguer pledged to return the country to order, normalcy, and reconstruction. He presented himself as a benevolent father figure, stern but paternalistic.

The result of the 1966 election was as expected. Balaguer won 57 percent of the vote to 39 percent for Bosch. The fact that nearly 40 percent of the electorate literally risked their lives to vote for a man who only campaigned three times out of his house attests to their bravery and to the continued support that Bosch, the PRD, and the liberal democracy commanded in the country. Nevertheless, it is important to stress that Balaguer did win by a landslide. The shy, unobtrusive bachelor had genuine support among certain sectors of Dominican society, including the peasants. Although Bosch and his supporters ignored or chose not to recognize it, Balaguer was not viewed by most Dominicans as an ogre or even a *trujillista*, but rather as a moderating influence necessary at a time of intense social and political division.

Balaguer's presidency, 1966–1978, was one of the most intriguing and in many respects one of the most successful in the country's political history. Balaguer defies easy characterization. Some see him as a cunning oppressor of the population, others view him as a tool of U.S. business, still others picture him as a crafty manipulator of the Dominican body politic. Balaguer is all of these – and more. He may best be described as a civilian caudillo. Unlike the gruff, macho, military men who have largely dominated the country since independence, Balaguer is quiet, a poet, ill-at-ease in front of the cameras and in large groups, not charismatic, hard-working, and personally honest. But beneath the quiet demeanor Balaguer was in complete control of the political system, taking instruction from neither his military chiefs nor the United States, confident and aggressive in the right circumstances, a pragmatic reformer, and, when necessary, a brutal repressor. Balaguer was both a nationalist and a cautious friend of foreign interests, a pragmatic politician and a wily strategist who knew all of Trujillo's tricks and more.

This mixture of outward modesty and inner strength and cunning served Balaguer remarkably well. He largely ignored or silenced his opposition and relegated it to the role of onlooker, while he moved ahead with vigorous economic revitalization. By 1970 Balaguer had consolidated his position and was firmly in command, overseeing an era of unprecedented economic prosperity largely fueled by U.S. assistance and commonly referred to as the "Dominican miracle." With sugar prices skyrocketing, foreign investment flowing in, tourism on the increase, and business, the military, and the middle class all content, the country moved forward with a sense of confidence and drive not seen since the height of the Trujillo era.

Balaguer's accomplishments were many, and he spared no effort in reminding the population of the gains made. These were all presented in highly personalistic terms. It was *his* dam, *his* agrarian reform, *his* housing projects, *his* schools, clinics, irrigation canals, and bridges. Through the constant public relations efforts of his administration, Balaguer was able to present his regime to the world in a favorable light. For domestic and international consumption the Dominican Republic was pictured as a nation of prosperity, stability, and great progress.

Beneath the hyperbole of Balaguer's public relations effort stood another perception of the "Dominican miracle." Under Balaguer, the unemployment rate remained high, at 30–40 percent, illiteracy was in the same vicinity, and most of the population remained locked in poverty and squalor. While per capita income rose dramatically, this was due chiefly to U.S. pump-priming; the distribution of income remained remarkably inequitable. Most of the new wealth was placed in the hands of the already wealthy and the new middle class; the standard of living of most of the rest of the population actually declined. Malnutrition remained widespread, infant mortality was high, and the social conditions of the poor, especially in the cities, deteriorated. These, plus the government's periodic support of right-wing terrorism directed against the PRD, led to another picture of the Dominican Republic – not of progress and democracy, as the government claimed, but of repression and oligopoly designed to serve the needs of the few while the majority went without.

The severe gap between the well-publicized "Dominican miracle" of Balaguer and the harsh realities of life for the Dominican lower class left the regime with its most serious problem. The government could hold onto power and intimidate the opposition as it did in the 1970 and 1974 elections, but it could never claim that it was popular. With the PRD sitting out the elections, Balaguer won handily, but huge segments of the electorate showed their sentiments by casting blank ballots.

With the Dominican economy supported by revenues from highly volatile sugar prices and sometimes fickle U.S. assistance programs, it was inevitable that the "miracle" would one day end. By 1970 most of the aid had dried up, and in 1974 OPEC oil price hikes, a decline in the world sugar market, increased balance-of-payments deficits, high inflation, and even more widespread unemployment, potentially threatened the stability of the Balaguer government. Added to the economic woes were numerous charges of military and bureaucratic corruption and heightened disgust with the repressive tactics used by the government.

Balaguer had once been able to revive a flagging government with the announcement of some new grand scheme or massive public works project, but now the aging and ill president began to flounder. Balaguer was no longer seen as an adroit manipulator who could fix everything. The Dominican people were being squeezed more and more – not just the poor, who had always suffered, but now a sizeable portion of the middle class, who had once formed the basis of Balaguer's support but increasingly demanded honesty, democracy, and a concern for the legitimate pleas of the lower classes.

With the regime demonstrating weakness, the opposition began to sense an opportunity. The PRD once more revived its rusting grass-roots organization. After being frustrated and intimidated for a decade, the PRD, under the leadership of moderate, millionaire rancher Antonio Guzmán, emerged as the social-democratic alternative to Balaguer.

The 1978 election thus became the first meaningful presidential contest in twelve years. Balaguer was clearly in trouble with the electorate, especially the middle class and the poor, and in Gúzman the PRD had a moderate, effective candidate acceptable to the Dominican oligarchy and the U.S. embassy.

The election provoked a major crisis. Not surprisingly, the military and conservative civilians saw Gúzman and the PRD as a threat to the status quo. Envisioning a shake-up of the high command, fewer opportunities for graft, and possibly an opening up to Havana, the military moved in to seize the ballot boxes and annul the election because the vote count showed Guzmán with an early lead.

Although the action of the armed forces was reminiscent of numerous past interventions in the democratic process, the situation now, in both the Dominican Republic and the United States, had changed. With considerable pressure from the Carter administration and threats of Dominicans to bring the country to a halt with a massive general strike, Balaguer convinced the military to return the seized ballot boxes and the count was resumed.

After what seemed an inordinately long delay and concessions granted to the *Balagueristas* that included giving them majority control in the Dominican Senate, Guzmán was named the winner with 832,319 votes, to 669,112 for Balaguer. World opinion, strong pressure from the Carter administration, and vigilance and direct actions by the Dominicans combined to save the democratic process.

Antonio Guzmán took office in August 1978, to lead the first social-democratic government since Bosch's short and unhappy tenure in 1963. Guzmán promised reform, justice, and freedom, and castigated the military for trying to thwart the vote. On hand at the inauguration were some thirty representatives of the United States who reinforced the position of the Carter administration in supporting democracy.

In office, Guzmán moved away from the practices of Balaguer by allowing more political freedom and human rights, stressing social programs for the poor, and putting tighter controls on foreign investment. The fact that he was a skilled administrator and moderate politician strengthened his position. In addition, the Dominican Republic is a different country now than it was twenty years ago: more prosperous, more middle class, more confident.

But the authoritarian strain also remains strong in the Dominican Republic, and it comes increasingly to the surface in times of crisis and economic downturn. Moreover, the long course of Dominican history surveyed here provides few precedents for stable democratic government. What may seem stable and lasting now in the Dominican Republic can, as stated in the provocative title of a book about the country by former ambassador John Bartlow Martin, be quickly "overtaken by events."

5

Social Structure and Social Groups

The Dominican Republic has had a sad and often tragic history. But what of the more fundamental social, economic, and political conditions that underlie this history and that have produced such an unfortunate legacy? The repeated incidents of domestic strife, foreign intervention, national and international breakdown, despotism and dependency that figure so prominently in Dominican history are in fact manifestations of more basic socioeconomic and sociopolitical problems that emanate from the very foundations of national life.

SOCIAL STRUCTURE

No single factor by itself is sufficient to explain the persistence of Dominican underdevelopment and its problems as a nation. But surely the prevailing class and social structure must be placed at or near the top of the list. The historic social and racial separation of the classes, the rigidities of the social structure, the two-class system, the emergence now of a middle class, and the growing polarization and potential for class warfare, are all essential factors in enabling us to understand the Dominican system – and the recent changes occurring therein.

Any discussion of the Dominican social structure is best begun by stating that the Dominican Republic is a deeply divided and unequal society. Vast gaps separate the classes, and the stark realities of class separation can be found everywhere – in clothes, housing, language, opportunities, jobs. As with many racially complex societies, these differences are both socioeconomic and racial.

Race and class are closely interrelated. Those at the top of the Dominican social pyramid tend to be white, of European background. Those at the bottom are not only poor but they tend also to be black, descendants of the original slaves or more recent arrivals from Haiti brought in to cut sugar cane. In between (and numerically the largest

51

group), is the mulatto population. Much of the new middle class comes from the mulatto element, though within this group there are both further sharp economic gradations and various racial subtypes.

The white elite has historically dominated the nation's social, political, and economic life. But there are avenues for ambitious poorer (and darker) individuals to rise in the social scale, chiefly through politics and the army. Those who attend diplomatic receptions in Santo Domingo will probably note that the civilian, banking, and (old) moneyed interests there will be white or light mulatto and will congregate on one side, while the military officers, generally darker, will congregate separately. But the military is also a route to wealth and power, and the Dominican Republic has thus had more black and mulatto presidents than any nation in the western Hispanic world. Yet it is a measure of the Dominicans' preoccupation with race that this is a statistic about which they have very ambiguous feelings.

From a cold statistical viewpoint, the class differences in the Dominican Republic are stark. Fifty percent of the population receives only 13 percent of the total income; in contrast, the highest 6 percent of the population receives 43 percent of the income. Although the gross national product (GNP) has boomed ahead in the last decade at rates of 5 percent per year, and GNP per capita is now about $850 per year (up from $250 in 1966), the statistics are misleading. Most of the new wealth has gone to the upper and middle classes, while 80 percent of the Dominican population remain in a situation of undernourishment and malnutrition.

With a minimum wage of fifty cents per hour in many economic enterprises (and far less in others where the minimum wage is not enforced), with wages in the agricultural sector averaging $3.50 per day (paid only on the days worked), and with an unemployment rate of about 30 percent (plus another 20 percent underemployed), it is clear that poverty is the situation of life for most of the Dominican population. Life for them is a real and constant struggle to provide the basic necessities of food, shelter, and clothing. Poverty is visible in the bloated bellies of many of the children, in the inadequate housing and health facilities, and in the diseased and malformed bodies of many adults.

While the prosperity of the Balaguer years has not led to an improvement in the standard of living of the poor (whose condition in life may have actually worsened during this period of "miracle" economic growth), the situation of the Dominican upper classes reveals a much different situation. They have been the chief beneficiaries of the "miracle." There are now several elites: an older gentry class, a business-commercial elite that emerged around the turn of the century, a new rich class associated with Trujillo, and an even newer rich elite whose wealth is in land, banking, the professions, light industry, and tourism. All these elites profited enormously from the Balaguer era.

The upper classes worry about things different from those at the pyramid's bottom. Whereas the latter must concern themselves with basics such as jobs, food, housing, and survival, the former focus on such issues as the world market price for sugar (critical to their and the country's wealth), the waxing and waning of U.S. power and investments (also crucial to this group's position), trade patterns, the future of tourism, family ties, and gossip. The perspectives of the upper classes are concentrated outwardly on their relations with their large North American neighbor, and internally on the need for order, discipline, and building a national infrastructure. Little talk about poverty or unemployment emanates from their plush homes in the western sectors of Santo Domingo, their farms in the Cibāo, and their vacation houses in the mountains.

The gap between rich and poor in the Dominican Republic thus involves more than money or economic statistics. It is an attitudinal gap between persons inhabiting entirely different worlds. For one group the concerns are immediate, basic, and tied to life-sustaining activities. For the other the concerns are wider, longer-range, involving broader worlds. These two worlds are far apart; they touch occasionally (the wealthy have maids and get their shoes shined), but they do not meet. These gaps imply not only a vast separation between the social classes but mean also, perhaps inevitably, the potential for class conflict. With little in common and so much distance between them, the upper and lower classes both sense that one day there will be war between them—that, as well as other uncomfortable facts of life, is usually covered over with characteristic Dominican politeness.

URBAN AND RURAL POVERTY

The sheer poverty of most of the population (perhaps 80 percent) is, to the visitor, the single most striking and immediate feature of the Dominican Republic. The tourist brochures that present the country as a romantic vacation playground or a step backward in time to the swashbuckling days of Columbus say nothing of the tin and wood shanties along Santo Domingo's Ozama River or the numerous poor neighborhoods that surround the city. In fact, along the beautiful stretch of the Caribbean that leads from the airport to the tourist hotels, the Dominicans have done a good job of hiding their poverty. Poverty is something to be ashamed of, to disguise so that foreigners will have a good impression.

Nonetheless, the poverty is stark, real, and plainly visible to all who care to see. In the poor neighborhoods there are open sewers, naked children with bloated bellies, unemployed young men, and always the forlorn gaze of poverty and malnutrition. To the poor urban dwellers a normal day includes the usually fruitless search for employment, endless hanging around, a continuous struggle to manage an insecure household in the face of accelerating price increases for such staples as rice and beans, constant shortages of basic foodstuffs, and a climate of despair and rising violence.

It is in the cities where the poverty seems most stark, particularly when seen against the most visible signs of modernity: new skyscrapers, vast building projects, ostentatiously displayed wealth. Such contrasts serve as a reminder of how much needs to be done in the Dominican Republic, and they indicate how unevenly modernity has come. The recent thrusts toward development and economic growth have largely passed by the urban poor, turning them into a vast army of disadvantaged who pose a major potential threat to the elite-dominated social and political structure. But these poor Dominicans are no longer passive; they have demonstrated and struggled for decent housing, a modicum of public services (water, electricity), and, most importantly, jobs. It is these barrio residents who brought Juan Bosch to power in 1962, who died in the aborted revolution of 1965, and who have on numerous occasions recently gone into the streets in protest.

The anomaly of the Dominican urban poor is that despite their political influence through the PRD, their great numbers, and their vast anger against the status quo, little change has come to the barrio. Despite the industrialization and economic stimulation of the Balaguer era, things remain the same for the poor – the housing situation and services have actually gotten worse. With a reformist PRD government installed in 1978, the urban poor eagerly awaited change and delivery on the many promises that the government must fulfill to hold the allegiance of the people who voted for it. But the problems are so enormous and the means of resolving them so limited that hope is wearing thin, cynicism abounds, and the potential for renewed violence is rising.

The poverty of the urban centers is starkly visible, creating severe tensions and periodic outbreaks of violence, but the rural peasant endures his poverty in a different setting and reveals his frustrations in a less overt manner. Rural poverty is less visible because the contrasts are not so great; it is also a poverty that is "quiet."

Campesinos live a simple life of hard work, few pleasures, and little hope of improvement. If they are lucky enough to own a small parcel of land (300,000 families own tracts of less than five acres), it is probably poor rocky land that barely yields a meagre subsistence, is inadequate for a family and gives insufficient surpluses to sell in the market. The chances are even greater that the campesino has no land at all, however, working occasionally as a tenant farmer or sugar cane harvester. The work is long and arduous, the pay extremely low, and protection against disability, old age, or unemployment nonexistent.

The Dominican Republic's statistics on illiteracy, unemployment, life expectancy, and per-capita income are dismally low when presented as *national* figures, but the situation in the countryside is actually far below the national average. Unemployment in the campo may be as high as 50 percent, illiteracy 80 percent, life expectancy at least ten years below the national figure, and incomes far below those in the urban areas.

The terrible poverty of the rural population has not yet led to the violence and class conflict that now seems endemic in the cities. There is an attitude of resignation to one's fate in the campo. The traditional paternalistic ties between landlord and peasant remain strong and greatly influence the character of politics. The peasant remains generally conservative, so far unattracted to appeals for guerrilla revolution. For example, in the 1965 revolution, the fighting was largely confined to the capital, while the countryside remained marginal to the conflict. In this regard, the urban and rural poor exhibit little solidarity in a class sense.

There are encouraging programs to bring social justice and new possibilities to the poor, and the situation in the Dominican Republic is not entirely without hope. The Guzmán government initiated new programs to provide low-cost housing and job training. In the rural areas both Balaguer and Guzmán introduced agrarian reform programs designed to modernize farming and to give land to landless peasants.

Despite these programs and the expenditure of millions of dollars, the process of bringing change to the poor in both urban and rural areas is terribly slow and strewn with countless roadblocks. The rapid industrialization of the last fifteen years has not had a significant impact on unemployment or lower-class incomes. Much of the industrial expansion has been capital- rather than labor-intensive. Although a new mining operation or semiconductor plant provides some jobs, the mass of uneducated and unskilled workers have not benefitted from these activities.

The pay schedule and the weakness of union organization also contribute to the failure to alleviate the conditions of poverty. With a minimum wage (unenforced) of fifty cents per hour (even less in the "free zones," where the new factories are), a worker can hardly feed his family, let alone keep up with rising inflation. Attempts by workers to raise pay scales by unionization are often met by resistance and intimidation on the part of owners and, under Balaguer, from the government as well. The weak labor organizations must compete with better-financed company unions and "sweetheart contracts" that weaken still further the union's bargaining power. The high unemployment also keeps the unions impotent by providing a virtually unlimited supply of unskilled workers on which employers can draw if their laborers get "uppity."

In the rural areas different roadblocks stand in the way of change. At the heart of the problem is the lack of sufficient arable land. Only about 50 percent of the total territory is arable. What arable land is available is not always used effectively. Many wealthy landowners, for example, prefer to keep their rich lands as pasture and not under cultivation, because cattle and vast lands are symbols of lordly status. Less than half of the rich Cibão Valley is under cultivation.

The intransigence of the landed elites lies at the hub of the country's frustrated efforts at agrarian reform. This, in turn, is reinforced by a centuries-long tradition which afforded social standing on the basis of the ownership of land. Land is viewed as both an economic investment and a source of social and political power. The lands inherited from Trujillo and once intended for agrarian reform, for example, have since been swallowed up by upwardly climbing government and military officials, who see the ownership of land as the symbol by which they will gain upper-class status. Generations of landlords are not easily convinced that their status must be sacrificed so as to defuse social tensions or attain a newly defined standard of social justice.

So far, attempts by the government to change the land system have not been successful. Bosch was overthrown in 1963 in part because of his land reform proposals. On numerous occasions angry landowners protested Balaguer's plans to limit the size of landholdings. Although the Balaguer government's agrarian reform efforts were quite limited, the strong reaction of owners even to the proposals of a conservative government indicates how sensitive the issue is. Balaguer settled for a much reduced program that gave provisional titles to peasants for unused government land of low quality.

The Guzmán government entered office with a renewed pledge to redress the inequalities of land ownership. But the president and his closest friends were themselves large landowners; hence the emphasis was on modernization of agriculture rather than much land redistribution. The Guzmán government pushed the development of agro-industry aimed at export crop diversification, which will weaken the dependence on sugar.

The efforts to effect social change and alleviate the problems of poverty and inequality are thus mired in complex, long-term social and power relationships, in the necessities of modern industrial development that call for a postponement of expensive social programs, and in decades, even centuries, of poverty and neglect. The Dominican lower

classes remain trapped in poverty with few possibilities for improvement. Government development strategies that seek to pull society forward by means of industrialization and the modernization of infrastructure may be sound policy at one level, but they have had little or even
deleterious impact on the 80 percent who remain untouched by the
economic "miracle" around them.

THE EMERGING MIDDLE CLASS: AGENT OF CHANGE?

The conditions of inequality existent between the 5 percent of the
population who enjoy wealth, status, and power, and the 80 percent who
live in abject poverty, is perhaps the most important and obvious feature
of the Dominican social structure. But sandwiched between these two
groups is a rising middle class, about 15 to 20 percent of the population,
whose political influence is now commensurate with its rising economic
power.

The role of the middle class in Latin America, however, remains
controversial. Is it a force for reaction or a force for democracy? The
answer is: it depends. The middle class generally favors modernization,
development, and democracy at a stage when it is trying to wrest control
from the old oligarchies and needs support in its quest from urban
workers. Once it has achieved power, however, the middle class has
tended to turn conservative, employing the military to keep the lower
classes in place.

In the Dominican Republic the middle class is small, but its importance is out of proportion to its size. Its ranks include government
workers, army officers, small businessmen, students, teachers, clerics,
doctors, lawyers, technicians, and professionals of all sorts. These are all
"influentials," the opinion-leaders. The middle sectors are dominant in
some of the most important national institutions: officer corps, Church,
bureaucracy, universities, political parties and trade union leadership.
Some would say the middle class has become the most important social
group in the country.

The era of prosperity under Balaguer helped expand the middle
class's ranks. Those who knew Santo Domingo in the 1960s will hardly
recognize the city today. New middle-class neighborhoods have sprouted
all around; the focus of business, commercial, social, even governmental
affairs has shifted from the old center to the suburbs; and a great variety
of movie houses, car dealerships, supermarkets, discothèques, and other
amenities of middle class existence have blossomed.

The middle class is diverse politically. Some of its members are
cautious about politics, some are apathetic. Many are conservative,
forming the opposition to Bosch in the early 1960s, the loyalist camp in

Artist with his sculpture

the 1965 revolution, and the early basis of support for the Balaguer government. But many others hold more liberal and democratic values. It was also from the middle class that support for Bosch's PRD came. And when Balaguer's government became too repressive and corrupt, the middle class abandoned it and went over to the opposition. In 1978, when the military sought to frustrate the popular electoral vote, it was these middle class businessmen, shopowners, doctors, and lawyers who protested the most.

The contradictions within the middle class are best explained by the diverse groups making up that sector. The upper-middle class, consisting of important businessmen and well-established professionals, tends to be most conservative, aspiring to or holding elitist values that the elites themselves no longer hold. High-ranking military officers (colonels and generals) also fall within this group. The middle-middle class, consisting of government planners and economists, teachers and university students, younger professionals and military officers, represents a more mixed group; they often favor reform and support the PRD, but some of their members are quite conservative. The lower-middle class is a swing group: its economic and social position is precarious, leading it to support stable and conservative causes; yet when corruption becomes so widespread that its normal activities suffer, this group can also swing to support reformist movements.

The great diversity of the middle class makes generalizations about its political behavior difficult. What can be said safely is that the middle class is growing and will exercise an increasingly important role in the national life. This is a relatively new development, first under Trujillo when a sizable middle class began to grow, and whose growth then accelerated during the prosperity and stability of the Balaguer years.

Not only is the middle class larger, but it has definite viewpoints on many political matters and its members have the controlling voice in most of the nation's institutions. However, the middle class still speaks with many voices, ranging from the far left to the far right. It is so deeply divided that one cannot speak of a middle-class society – stable, moderate, middle-of-the-road – emerging as yet in the Dominican Republic. Thus, whether this middle class will evolve as a stabilizing influence, as U.S. officials fervently hope, or will continue as a divided *and* divisive element, cannot at this stage be clearly ascertained.

CLASS AND CLASS CONFLICT

The Dominican Republic is a nation deeply fragmented along class and racial lines. Because the 1965 revolution was both a political and a class revolt that was frustrated and remains unfinished, many observers have predicted an imminent renewal of the struggle. Yet the defeat of the constitutionalists and the restoration of elite and bourgeois rule under Balaguer did not usher in a period of renewed conflict. There have been occasional flare-ups against price increases, police brutality, and fraudulent electoral practices, but the disturbances have been isolated and have not involved any sustained class challenges to the system. Why?

The relative absence of social and class conflict in the Dominican Republic since 1965 can be analyzed from a variety of perspectives. One view commonly expressed by moderates and conservatives is that life for the general population has not been all that bad. The country, it is said, has returned to a climate of normalcy where social and political antagonisms have been put aside in favor of a concerted effort to achieve economic development. The proponents of the normalcy position see the 1965 uprising as an aberration instigated by a small group of malcontents. They say the historical legacy, cultural foundations, and psychological makeup of the Dominicans are not conducive to large-scale social unrest. The paternalistic and patron-client-centered concept of politics, and the deep-seated respect for traditional social relationships, militate against class conflict. The normalcy reigning since 1965 is then a reflection of the *real* Dominican Republic. This argument asserts that the spirit of politeness, gentleness, cooperation, respect for authority, and resigned acceptance of adversity serve as safeguards against destructive class warfare.

There is considerable truth in these arguments, but it is by no means the whole truth. Dominicans *are* conditioned by their historical and cultural tradition and they are, like the rest of us, creatures of habit. But they are also very pragmatic. Lacking arms and an organizational base, it is quite prudent for the Dominican lower classes to remain quiescent for now. Martyrdom for some presumably glorious cause may be attractive to the young, but not to those who are older or have families to provide for. To them it makes no sense to get killed if there is no chance of success; a better strategy is patience, forbearance, waiting for an opportunity (as in 1965) when the possibility of winning is greater.

Another very concrete reason for the general social calm since 1965 has to do with the weakness of the left groups in the Dominican Republic, and government repression of them. Since 1961, when the political system was opened up, the left and Marxist groups have enjoyed little popular support. One can find Marxist groups in the country, but their political influence has been small. Poorly led and lacking organization, they have not had the strength to challenge, let alone take over, a government. After the revolution, when leftist groups like the Fourteenth of June Movement, the Dominican Popular Movement

(MPD), and the Communist Party either disbanded, went into exile, or were suppressed, there were few who lamented their eclipse. And when some of these same groups sought to foment guerrilla warfare in the Dominican countryside, they were unable to mobilize popular support and were eventually snuffed out by the military. Popular disinterest and government repression have kept the far left weak and divided.

The Dominicans have not generally explained their plight in Marxian terms, unlike their neighbors in Cuba, Jamaica (for a time), Nicaragua, and Grenada. The situation is changing, especially among educated youth, where Marxism has become *the* framework in which political and economic discussion takes place. But today, if there is any fervent ideological sentiment among the people, it is generally expressed in terms of a quest for liberal democracy. The conflicts in the Dominican Republic have not been aimed at achieving Marxian socialism; rather, they have been directed toward achieving democratic and constitutional government, respect for basic human rights, and more traditional liberal precepts.

Still another reason for the absence of manifest class conflict in the Dominican Republic is the continuing influence of personalistic politics. The history of the Dominican Republic has been one of conflict more between strong leaders than between rival ideologies. This is changing, but leadership, or the perceived absence thereof, is still crucial for explaining the ups and downs of national politics. Strong leaders provide continuity, unity, and stability – for a time; weak leaders invite movements directed against them. The 1965 revolution was not just an ideological and class conflict; it was also an effort to restore coherence and leadership and to replace the floundering and ineffective Donald Reid Cabral.

The "leadership principle" also helps explain the continuing popularity of former president Joaquín Balaguer. Despite the repression, onerous austerity programs, high unemployment, and blatant favoritism to the moneyed classes that marked his presidency, Balaguer remained a popular figure even to the lower classes. He did not rule by force alone. He was respected as an efficient administrator, an honest man, a decent individual, and, despite his meek appearance, a strong leader. He was defeated in the 1978 election not just on political and ideological grounds, but also because his health was failing and he was seen as a leader who could no longer keep control.

Although the grounds for class conflict and social unrest are present in the Dominican Republic, there are other factors tending to militate against a violent upheaval. The catalyst that might set off the conflagration is often hard to pinpoint; the Dominicans are not easily aroused to violent tactics. They have, historically, been a conservative people influenced strongly by traditional social relationships, beliefs, and forms of leadership. Some of them are Marxists but few have become Leninists or Stalinists.

It would be a grave miscalculation, however, to conclude that the chances of future violence and upheaval are minimal. The frustrations that breed on poverty, inequality, and injustice are many and profound. Although presently latent, violence could explode again as it did in 1965. If and when such violence comes, it will likely be used with great reluctance, probably as a result of some disruption of national leadership, and only after great provocation. But surely one of the lessons of the 1965 revolution is that when provoked, the Dominican people will fight to the death.

GROUP DYNAMICS AND THE DOMINICAN SOCIAL SYSTEM

Dominican society is sharply divided horizontally in terms of the several classes present. For this reason it is absolutely necessary that one employs class analysis to help explain the nation's politics and political economy. But Dominican society is also structured vertically, in terms of occupational, functional, and power groups. Both perspectives are necessary in order to understand the workings of the system.

Dominican politics is often dominated by the interplay of key power contenders and corporate groups. These include family and kinship groups, the army, the Church, the economic elites, students, labor, and the Americans. These groups form a patchwork of contending factions and interest groups acting and interacting on the basis of self-interest, moral or ideological principle, or simply raw power. We shall be looking at each of these major groups in turn.

Family and Kinship Groups

Family and kinship (extended family) groups are still very important in the Dominican Republic. Who is related to whom, who is the godfather of whom, who owes whom what kinds of favors – these are all important questions to the Dominicans; these questions are also critical in shaping the national political system. Clean versus dirty business deals, social and family slights, what one person's grandfather did to another person's grandfather – these can be issues of major national importance. Particularly in a country where everyone who counts knows everyone else or is interrelated, such personal and family relations take on major importance.

What is often covered over with the language of partisan or ideological conflict may be more basically the expression of such conflicts between rival families. Political parties, at least the traditional ones, are often just family cliques devoid of genuine program or ideological differences. Similarly, the complex interrelations between civilian and military elites are often governed more by family ties or patronage connections than by policy differences.

Foreigners on brief visits to the Dominican Republic often have a hard time sorting out what goes on in front of the Dominican curtain from what goes on behind it. The former is visible, public, for the world to see; the latter is private, hidden, secretive. Those who stay there longer come to realize that behind the partisan and ideological conflicts that are public is a web of family and personal relations that are private. To really understand Dominican politics one must come to grips with these family, kinship, and interpersonal relations, as well as with the more manifest and visible interest-group dynamics.

The Military

Among organized groups, there is no question that the military holds the balance of power in the country. Recalling Dominican history should be sufficient to indicate how often power has rested in the hands of the generals.

At first glance the military would not appear to be such an imposing force. It numbers 28,300 men: 11,000 in the Army, 3,800 in the Navy, 3,500 in the Air Force, and 10,000 in the National Police. Its budget is about 10 percent of total public expenditures. The Dominican armed forces are much smaller and less well equipped than neighboring Cuba's, and their share of the budget is considerably less than it was in Trujillo's time and in the 1960s.

The manpower and budget figures, however, do not reflect the military's power. Its purpose is not so much to defend the nation's frontier and beaches from foreign aggressors as to serve as an internal occupation force and political instrument. Although the Dominican Republic has been governed almost continuously by civilian leaders since Trujillo's death in 1961, every government has been on probation to the military, and must recognize realistically the military's capacity to seize power. The military is always in the background, not necessarily seeking power, but adamant that power be wielded in a manner that does not threaten its prerogatives or destabilize the fragile sociopolitical order.

The military's strength and influence forces presidents to play a dangerous game of political manipulation. Balaguer and Guzmán both saw fit to shuffle military officers in and out of command or governmental posts in order to weaken their ability to plot against the administration. Payoffs and cushy opportunities for enrichment may also be given the officers. Balaguer was a master at playing this game, a fact that helps explain his longevity in office.

Guzmán also realistically recognized the military's power. After assuming office he retired twenty-three senior officers and 243 noncommissioned officers in an attempt to get rid of the potentially disloyal pro-Balaguer group. The key man that he replaced was General Enrique Pérez y Pérez, a Balaguer loyalist who had been also linked to the death squads operating in the early 1970s. Pérez was offered the ambassadorship to Spain and an attaché's position in London. After rejecting both, Pérez retired with a hefty pension; he made a commitment that he would stay out of politics.

But efforts to depoliticize the military can never be complete. The armed forces are a political agency and their officers are divided into groups with partisan objectives. There are pro-Balaguer, pro-Guzmán, and other factions. There are also splits between the services, between junior and senior officers, between conservatives and modernizers. Other officers are interested chiefly in lucrative contraband or business activities for themselves. A prudent president must walk a tightrope between these contending factions. Rumors of coups and coup preparations occur frequently. In 1979, Guzmán nipped in the bud a coup attempt by a group of disgruntled officers, but the incident served as a reminder of the tenuousness of the civilian government's position.

The Church

The Dominican Catholic Church is not as strong a force as it once was. Understaffed, not wealthy, with few programs, the Church cannot exert strong pressure. Despite the fact that the Dominican Republic is a Catholic country and its educational, social, and political institutions are infused by precepts of Catholic culture, the Church as a political agency is not very powerful.

The Church served for a long time as a prop of the Trujillo regime, and in earlier days its voice in telling parishioners how to vote was influential. It was identified with reactionary and conservative causes. But the Church has modernized itself and can no longer be identified automatically with the status quo. It does not have the personnel or the resources to be more than a secondary voice in national politics, and as the Dominican Republic has become more secular and middle class, its influence has diminished further. The Church is still influential on some issues–divorce, population control–but it is significant that the Dominican Republic has both an official family-planning program and legislation that has made the country a haven for "quickie" divorces.

The voice of the Church is still important, but it is no longer part of the old triumvirate of power (Church, Army, oligarchy), and in comparison with other groups its influence is no longer decisive.

Economic Elites

While the Church's influence has diminished over time, that of the economic elites has increased. Particularly as the nation has modernized, become more affluent, and involved itself more in international markets, the power of business groups has correspondingly increased.

The Dominican Republic is no longer governed by a small landed oligarchy. Rather, the landed oligarchy has also gone into business, and meanwhile a whole new class of bankers, industrialists, financiers, factory owners, managers, owners of commercial establishments, and importers-exporters has appeared. In 1963 the business groups were influential in overthrowing Bosch's democratic government, but today their numbers and influence are even greater than they were then.

The economic elites are organized into a Chamber of Commerce and associations of industry, commerce, and landowners. They are wealthy, often well educated, and always well connected. Especially under Balaguer they had direct pipelines into the government and received the advantage of advance knowledge of pending government economic decisions. Their influence is great not just because they are well connected but because the whole nation is dependent on them for jobs, financial expertise, and continuing prosperity. It is said in the Dominican Republic that the military is the ultimate arbiter of national politics, but the economic elites run the country on an everyday basis.

Students

University students must sometimes be reckoned with in Dominican politics, but their power is not nearly as great as that of the armed forces or the economic elites.

There are now 60,000 students enrolled in five universities in the country. The center of student activity is the Autonomous University of Santo Domingo (UASD), which has 27,000 students. By most standards of judgment the UASD is woefully underfunded and is too intimately tied up with the nation's political turmoil.

The students come overwhelmingly from the middle class. Many of them want to use their education as a means to get ahead and to share in the growing affluence of the country. They are often impatient with or indifferent to politics; seeing the university as an escalator for upward mobility, they have helped depoliticize the campus since the great upheavals in the 1960s.

Other students remain highly political, and the university is their training ground. The activists are divided between PRD, Social-Christian, and various communist and far-left factions. Frequently they keep the university and the capital city in turmoil. The students led the

A building at the Autonomous University of Santo Domingo

protests against the repression of the Balaguer government. In retaliation the police and military units entered the university grounds and fired indiscriminately at the students. Fearing the adverse publicity from such actions, the government next sought to "starve" the University by drastically reducing its budget. These actions further enraged the students, who touched off renewed confrontations.

The university students, sometimes reinforced by high school students, often constitute the most visible counterforce to governmental power, and they are particularly active against repressive regimes. They serve as national spokesmen on such issues as freedom, democracy, repression, and social justice. Through the Dominican Student Federation (FED), they often keep at center stage political issues that other groups are content to ignore. By themselves the students cannot topple a government, but they can certainly embarrass one. In alliance with such groups as organized labor and some discontented military officers and elements from the middle class, they have the potential to help lead a radical movement, as in the 1965 revolution.

With a democratic government inaugurated in 1978, the universities returned to a level of peace. But their importance remains. First, they provide important technical training that the country desperately needs. Second, they are a major and sometimes last bastion of contrary ideas. Third, they are the major source of national political leadership. Whatever their problems, academic or political, the universities and their student bodies remain vigilant.

Organized Labor

The Dominican labor movement has had its ups and downs. Suppressed by Trujillo, it emerged as a significant force for the first time in the 1960s. Persecuted again during the period of the revolution and its aftermath, and tightly regulated and controlled under Balaguer, the unions have recently begun to make another comeback.

Since the 1960s there have been four major labor groups: communist, PRD, Social-Christian, and U.S. embassy-sponsored. The PRD and Social-Christian unions have been the most successful, though the communists have made gains in some unions. The embassy-sponsored unions are looked on as foreign agencies, but they are the beneficiaries of American money and therefore have achieved some success.

The unions have traditionally been weak and divided. They have few funds. Their organizational and training programs are limited. Employers buy them off or use the police to intimidate them. The unemployment rate is so high that employers know they can easily replace workers who seek to unionize. Government restrictions on union activities are so rigid that it is virtually impossible to organize a legal strike in the Dominican Republic.

With a sympathetic social-democratic government installed in the National Palace in 1978, the situation of the unions began to improve. The unions have also unified their command under a single General Confederation of Labor. But organized labor is still a comparatively weak force in the Dominican Republic, often intimidated by the military or employers, not able to compete with well-financed company unions, forced to accept sweetheart contracts, and certainly no match for the more powerful employer interests.

The situation of unorganized labor is even more dismal. The large *lumpenproletariat* of the capital city, as we have seen, lives in miserable conditions with no organization or laws to protect it. Its members formed some of the "shock troops" in the 1965 civil war; they were also its chief victims.

The rural peasantry—still roughly half the population—is also unorganized and therefore powerless. There are a few farm cooperatives and peasant leagues, but the formation of a strong national peasants' association begun under Bosch was ruled out by his successors. Numerically the country's largest group, the peasantry is simply not a force that counts for much in Dominican national politics.

The American Presence

The United States is a major actor in the Dominican Republic, not just in terms of the country's international trade and relations but in its internal politics as well. It may safely be said that along with the military and the economic elites, the United States is a major domestic political force – and not necessarily ranked in that order.

There are some 9,000 Americans living and working in the Dominican Republic. This is a small number in comparison with the Dominican population, but it is extremely influential. The Americans are concentrated in banking and commercial concerns, in the several large multinationals operating in the country, in religious and educational institutions, and in the U.S. embassy. The latter is a major hub of Dominican national politics.

The United States government has been deeply involved in Dominican internal affairs at least since the turn of the century. One need only recall the two long military occupations during this period, and the almost constant meddling of the United States in Dominican affairs during more "normal" times. Although the American influence has waxed and waned, the Dominican Republic can be thought of as a dependency, a satellite – almost a colony of the United States. Private capital, foreign aid, technical assistance, military training missions, and the long arms of its embassy give the United States a vast range of levers with which to manipulate the Dominican Republic. American officials in the Dominican Republic often act more as proconsuls than as the representatives of one sovereign state to another.

The heavy hand of the United States in the Dominican Republic has, strangely, seldom been the subject of widespread resentment. The U.S. intervention in 1965 generated considerable anti-Americanism, and there is some resentment of American company officials who cluster into compounds with their own exclusive supermarkets and clubs. But many Dominicans continue to look on the United States as a *patrón* and protector, a dispenser of aid and technology – a source of inspiration as well as consternation. Additionally, adept Dominican politicians have learned to manipulate the United States just as the United States manipulates them.

In recent years the relations between Dominicans and Americans have suffered some strains. The disclosure that the Gulf and Western Company reneged on payments to the Dominican government of millions of dollars in sugar futures prompted renewed talk of nationalizing Gulf and Western holdings. Revelations that the Philip Morris Company bribed members of the Balaguer government did not sit well with the Dominicans. The Dominicans have also been pursuing a more independent foreign policy recently, and seem determined to sever some of their dependency ties with the United States.

But the basic facts of life are that the Dominicans are still strongly dependent on the Americans and that the United States maintains a strategic hold on the nation's economic and political life. It is not likely that the United States will quickly relinquish that hold. Realistic Dominicans recognize that fact, and adjust accordingly.

What is likely is some modest readjustment of the terms of dependency and of the role of the United States in their country. The United States now has fewer official personnel there and less aid than in the last twenty years; consequently, it has fewer official levers to manipulate. That, however, did not stop the Americans from putting pressure on Balaguer and the military in 1978 to allow the vote count to proceed to a democratic outcome. But while the official American presence has been somewhat diminished, the private one has been increased, in the form of large American multinational corporations. The American presence thus remains a strong one in the Dominican Republic, but the form it takes is different and, as we shall see, the whole international context in the Caribbean is also undergoing alteration.

Power in the Dominican Republic remains imbalanced. It is concentrated in the hands of the few, not the many. That was clear in our discussions of both the class and social structure and the relative power of the social and interest groups. A decided inequality of wealth and political strength persists. Clearly, the most important groups in internal Dominican politics are the armed forces, the economic elites, and the Americans. Of secondary importance are the Church, the students, and the organized labor movement. Of almost no consequence at all, at least politically, are the largest groups numerically: the urban slum dwellers and the peasants. Hence, while the foundations for a more pluralistic and democratic system in the Dominican Republic have been laid, that process is still in its early stages and remains incomplete.

6

The Economy

The Dominican Republic has always been a country of passionate politics, intense interpersonal relations, and constant preoccupation with class and status issues. But more recently, as the country has modernized, economic issues have come to the fore. One should not go so far as to say economics has replaced politics as the major national preoccupation, but such a statement would not be too far from the truth.

FROM POLITICS TO POLITICAL ECONOMY

In the early 1960s, following Trujillo's death, the Dominican Republic had become a highly politicized nation. There were new parties, new ideologies, new political groups and movements, new policies and international concerns. The country experienced a sudden explosion of political mobilization. This period of high political intensity reached a crescendo in the 1965 revolution.

But since 1965 some dramatic changes have occurred: The country has been depoliticized; ideological and partisan passions have declined; politicians and political programs have yielded center stage to economists, managers, businessmen, technicians, and economic development plans. The attention of the Dominican people is less on the political divisions of the past than on getting ahead and stimulating further economic growth, for themselves and for the nation.

Economic development is now talked about in passionate terms. Political leaders who once debated intensely over various constitutional clauses, ideologies, and political party programs, are now preoccupied with foreign loan opportunities, balance of payments deficits, industrial free zones, and the price of sugar. This is not to suggest politics has disappeared from the Dominican Republic, but it is to say that the economy and all facets of it are becoming the primary focus. The country has

Making rope

come full circle from the intensely political years of the early 1960s. For the moment (a very important qualifier!), the Dominican Republic has put aside some of its earlier political conflicts in favor of a long agenda of economic development priorities. Issues of political economy now command more attention than those of pure politics.

The major objective of the Dominican Republic in this new era is to move away from its earlier status as an underdeveloped, dependent, single-crop economy that relies heavily on export earnings and employment derived from this single crop. In place of this "mono-economy" the Dominicans are working to create an economy in which the sources of income and the modes of production are diversified and control of the country's economic future is more in the hands of the Dominicans themselves than dependent on any single foreign importer, i.e., the United States. To that end the Dominicans are working strenuously to build an economy based on a healthy mixture of light industry, mining, tourism, and a modernized agricultural sector, which together will increase growth and lessen the dependence on sugar and the uncertainty of fluctuating world prices.

The consequences of the Dominicans' historic dependence on sugar

Workers shipping sugar cane to the processing mill

should be emphasized. Fluctuations in the price of sugar have made and unmade Dominican governments for generations. Because the country is so overwhelmingly dependent on its earnings from sugar, a price drop of as little as a few cents per pound can spell ruin for the Dominican economy. Also, if American sugar beet producers form a powerful lobby to keep out foreign sugar, or if the House Agricultural Committee, which sets import quotas, decides to give a higher quota to Cuba or the Philippines—any of these steps can be disastrous for the Dominicans. Or suppose American consumers decide to drink light beer instead of sugared beer or to use saccharine or other sugar substitutes in their coffee or soft drinks—that can also ruin the Dominican economy. Given such uncertainties and their dependence on markets over which they have no control, the Dominican need to diversify is imperative.

The push for diversification and economic independence will not be easy. The Dominican export dependency also helps perpetuate other dependency relationships. The country must also look to foreign sources for capital, energy, and industrial technology. Without these, the Dominicans cannot hope to modernize. Like many Third World nations, the Dominican Republic is caught between its desire for greater economic independence and its reliance on foreign capital, markets, resources, investment, and technology, in order to develop.

Hence the transition from an underdeveloped, dependent, single-crop economy to a more independent and diversified one will not be immediate. There are both older and newer forms of dependency. While the Dominicans are seeking to lessen their dependence on sugar, they remain absolutely dependent on outside sources for their petroleum. And while they are seeking to diversify their trade, they are still dependent on foreign markets to sell their products. It is in this context of transition and changing dependency relationships that we will discuss the Dominican economy.

THE EXPORT SECTOR

To understand the nature of the Dominican economy, one must examine the traditional export sector and the manner in which it influences the present economic situation. The Dominican Republic has been and continues to be a country whose agricultural production is the major source of export revenues. Nearly two-thirds of the country's export earnings derive from agriculture. Sugar and sugar by-products by themselves account for one-third of total export earnings and about one-third of the national employment. Coffee, cocoa, and tobacco account for another 30 percent of exports.

Although these staples account for over 60 percent of the national export earnings, recent developments in mining and light industry have helped provide greater diversity in the economy. Mining (gold, silver, bauxite, and particularly ferronickel) now accounts for 25 percent of national exports, a figure that has been rising steadily since 1970. Exports from the light industrial sector (clothing, electronic equipment, leather goods, textiles, industrial staples) account for the remaining 12–25 percent of foreign earnings.

The dependent character of the Dominican export sector and the serious problems resulting from such dependency can be illustrated by a brief look at trade statistics. Data for 1979 show that exports generated $675.5 million in revenue, with the United States being the chief purchaser (68 percent) and the Western European countries accounting for most of the rest. The Dominican Republic is thus heavily dependent on its continued ability to sell its products in the United States.

Even more troublesome for the Dominicans are the figures on the import side. In 1979, the Dominican Republic's imports totaled $859.2 million, primarily for fuel, machinery, chemicals, cars, and foodstuffs, and chiefly imported from the United States (50 percent), Japan, and West Germany (10 percent each). The Dominican Republic was left with

The western hemisphere's largest gold mine (Pueblo Viejo)

A ferronickel plant at Bonao

a trade deficit of $183.7 million. The deficit was due largely to declining export earnings for agricultural and mineral products, coupled with the familiar rise in prices for petroleum products and for manufactured goods. Income from sugar and sugar by-products dropped 13.5 percent in 1979 as a result of low world prices; ferronickel sales dropped by $20 million as a result of declining demand. Although tobacco prices and those of other Dominican mining products increased, it was insufficient to offset the downturn in the two major export products.

The decline in export earnings had a ripple effect on the entire economy. The government took in $32 million less than expected as a result of collecting less in export taxes. Declining sugar and nickel prices came at a time of sharply rising demand and higher prices for imported oil. In 1976, with sugar prices at their lowest, revenues from the sale of sugar were still sufficient to cover 100 percent of the cost of oil imports. In 1979, even with sugar prices increasing, total sugar revenues covered only 60 percent of oil costs. Rising balance of payments problems and increasing indebtedness were the results.

The declining world price for the products the Dominican Republic exports and steadily rising oil prices have also had a devastating effect on the domestic economy. The days of the "Dominican miracle," when the gross national product rose an average of 9–10 percent per year, are gone. The GNP is still rising and is currently at about $5 billion, but the growth rates of the boom years in the early 1970s will be difficult to achieve again.

Inflation has also become a major problem. Although the rate of inflation in 1979 was only 4 percent, in 1978 it was 12 percent and in 1980 around 16 percent. A continuing increase in oil prices will send it skyrocketing. What has held it down to moderate levels so far has been the Dominicans' ability to cut down the importation of foodstuffs and rely more on internal production. In 1979, for the first time, the Dominicans became self-sufficient in rice and beans, the two main staples of their diet.

The extent that the Dominican Republic relies on export earnings to stimulate growth is only one aspect of the dependency situation found in the economy. The increasing reliance on foreign investment provides another illustration. As President Guzmán stated in 1979, "My government considers that foreign investment is essential for our economic development and for achieving the transfer of technology which is so much needed by developing countries such as ours."

The Guzmán position was simply a restatement of Balaguer's policy. Since 1966 the Dominican Republic has become an attractive country for foreign investment. The heaviest foreign investment has been in the agricultural and foodstuffs sector, but recently there have been noticeable increases in mining, finance (insurance, banking and real estate), tourism, and light industry.

The major source of foreign investment capital is the United States. There are currently 125 subsidiaries of U.S. firms operating in the Dominican Republic. The largest by far is Gulf and Western, which has over $200 million invested in sugar refineries, real estate, hotels, and numerous other enterprises. Other major corporations include Colgate Palmolive, Philip Morris, Alcoa, Esso, 3M, Gillette, and Xerox.

The heavy involvement of these private companies, in particular the U.S.-based multinationals, has created both opportunities and problems. The Dominican Republic needs the capital, jobs, and technical skills these companies provide. But the costs are also considerable. The companies can often mobilize more money, lawyers, and influence than the entire Dominican government. They have not been above bribing Dominican military officials to maintain "labor peace" or legislators to achieve passage of favorable bills. Many Dominicans fear the country is being sold out to the multinationals. Dominican government and party leaders on all sides are determined to reorder the existing arrangements with foreign investors.

The changing nature of foreign investment in the Dominican

Republic and the nationalistic reaction to the dependency it engenders is best presented by examining the recent negotiations of the government with both Rosario Resources and Gulf and Western. In 1979 the Guzmán administration announced that the Dominican Republic had negotiated the purchase of Rosario Dominicano, making the country the owner of the largest open-pit gold mine in the Western Hemisphere. The $70 million paid to Rosario Resources of New York and Simplot Industries of Boise, Idaho, signalled the government's desire to secure control of this major national resource. The negotiations were cordial and not marred by major threats from the two sides. In fact, through a joint venture, the government had already acquired 46 percent of the Rosario stock; now it had control.

The relations with Gulf and Western have not been so happy. In the minds of many Dominicans, Gulf and Western provides a classic example of a rapacious, expansionist, power- and money-hungry conglomerate running roughshod over the interests of a small and weak country. Although Gulf and Western's holdings are diverse, the centerpiece is the sugar complex at La Romana. Foreign ownership of the country's prime sugar lands and of its largest refinery, in a country so heavily dependent on sugar, is only part of the problem. Gulf and Western has also been accused of bribery, union-busting, repressive tactics against political foes, influence-peddling, and a host of other sins. It has stimulated animosity that cuts across party and ideological lines. As one conservative Dominican businessman put it, "Gulf and Western is a monster that will take whatever we have."

Calls for the nationalization of Gulf and Western are common. Allegations by the Securities and Exchange Commission in the United States that Gulf and Western had failed to pay millions of dollars it owed the Dominican government added fuel to the nationalization movement. But Dominican officials insist they do not wish to nationalize Gulf and Western, only to work out a new relationship with it. They feel a more equitable arrangement can be reached to encourage Gulf and Western to expand its investments and channel some of them in socially useful ways. It is clear the Dominicans want and need such investment capital, but whether they will continue to put up with the giant multinational's more nefarious activities is uncertain. Obviously, the future of Gulf and Western in the Dominican Republic is precarious.

The discussion above makes it clear that the dependent economic position of the Dominican Republic is due chiefly to its relationship with the United States. About two-thirds of Dominican exports go to the United States, about half of its imports come from the United States, and hundreds of millions of investment dollars come principally from U.S.-based multinationals. Much of the time and energy of Dominican government and business leaders is consumed managing or coping with these complex relations, or seeking to negotiate new and fairer relationships. The Dominicans cannot change the fact that they are a small and dependent nation, but they can diversify to a certain extent and renegotiate some terms of their dependency.

Because the heart of the Dominican Republic's economic ties with the United States and the source of many of its problems involve trade and markets, both the Balaguer and Guzmán administrations sought to fashion policies that addressed declining export revenues, balance of payments deficits, rising indebtedness, and restrictive import barriers. The key issues, for the Dominicans, involve commodity price stabilization (especially the price of sugar), government subsidies of U.S. sugar producers, and trade liberalization and the lowering of tariff barriers on Dominican exports. The Dominicans want to redefine and restructure existing relations with the United States so that the U.S. will import more, pay a fair price for what it imports, and be willing to provide aid and long-term cheap credit to a country in dire need of modernization.

From the Dominican viewpoint, what is required is greater opportunity to sell their products in the United States at an advantageous price. In the past, this has involved primarily sugar sales. Due to U.S. import quotas, import fees, the setting of quotas for each sugar-producing nation for obscure political or cold-war purposes, or subsidies of domestic sugar beet growers to reduce import demand, the Dominicans have long had to face constant uncertainty about the sale of their major export product. This uncertainty, as well as the highly unstable world market price for sugar, has created a "roller coaster" economy that is up when external demand and world prices are favorable, and down with disastrous consequences when external demand and world prices are constrained.

Although the major source of concern to Dominicans is available sugar markets and a stable (i.e., high) world price, the recent expansion of the Dominican industrial base to include textiles, clothing, leather goods, and additional agricultural foodstuffs has created greater pressure to achieve more equitable trading arrangements in these areas also. To that end the Dominicans have participated in the Generalized System of Preferences, which allows duty-free entry into the United States of certain selected products. In 1978, sixty-five Dominican products (about 25 percent of the items exported from the country) were allowed duty-free access to U.S. markets. Following the recent Geneva round of trade negotiations, the Dominican Republic and the United States signed a bilateral agreement giving greater access to American markets for Dominican textiles and clothing.

Even with these positive signs on the trading front, especially for these nontraditional exports, the key problem remains sugar markets and sugar prices. To illustrate, in 1974 and 1975 the price of sugar in the world market soared from ten cents per pound to seventy-six cents, creating a boom for the Dominican economy. Much of Balaguer's vaunted "miracle" was based on these high sugar prices and the earnings they generated. By 1978 sugar prices had plummeted again to seven cents, and then increased once again in 1979 to sixty-four cents. Not only was the world price in 1978 depressed, thus dropping the bottom out of the Dominican economy, but domestic growers in the United States were effectively pressing for fewer imports. It seemed unlikely that the most recent sugar boom would continue indefinitely.

The Dominican solution to the sugar dilemma has been to push vigorously for the International Sugar Agreement. The agreement, if signed by the United States and also by the European Common Market, would greatly aid in stabilizing prices and opening current barriers to foreign sugar. Action on the agreement is bogged down in Congress, however, where U.S. sugar producers have lobbied effectively to stall passage. In lieu of the International Sugar Agreement, the Dominicans have sought a bilateral agreement with the United States. After extensive negotiations, the United States agreed to reduce some import fees on sugar.

GOVERNMENT PROGRAMS TO STRENGTHEN THE ECONOMY

The Dominican effort to redefine, restructure, and reform its present condition of economic underdevelopment and dependency is an enormous, some would say impossible, task. The significant achievements of a more diversified economy and new trade arrangements have been more than offset by the burgeoning costs of OPEC oil and the continued depressed price of many commodities. Rather than diminishing or disappearing as the country modernizes and rearranges its trade relationships, dependency seems only to take on new forms. The desire to transform the economy is thus fraught with disappointment and frustration. Change is slow and often imperceptible; many features of the Dominican vicious circles of underdevelopment seem immune to change.

Yet the Dominicans are unified in their desire to take the necessary steps to expand trade, stimulate diversification, reduce underdevelopment, increase investments, control oil price-related inflation, and expand the country's economic base. To achieve both greater independence and modernization, the Dominican government has undertaken a number of initiatives.

Export Promotion

Although the Dominican government is actively seeking to renegotiate existing trade and price arrangements with the United States, it has also taken numerous steps on its own to expand the markets for Dominican goods. A new government agency, the Dominican Center for the Promotion of Exports (CEDOPEX), has been created to aid local businesses seeking expanded markets for their products. CEDOPEX provides three major services: (1) training programs to assist Dominican businessmen in gaining access to foreign markets; (2) market research to determine the potential sales of goods in foreign countries; and (3) overseas marketing offices. CEDOPEX maintains offices in the Caribbean, Latin America, and the United States, to assist Dominicans seeking to expand their exports.

A report by the CEDOPEX office in New York indicates the increasing success of these export efforts. In 1974, 110 nontraditional Dominican exports were sold in New York; by 1978 the number had increased to 288, an annual increase for those four years of 36 percent. One of the major reasons for the increase in Dominican products sold in New York is the increasing Dominican (and Hispanic) population in the city, who consume such Dominican products as canned beans, guava, mangoes, frozen coconut meat, beer, and honey.

Public Investment

Perhaps the most visible signs of economic development in the Dominican Republic are the numerous publicly funded construction projects. The government has made a firm commitment to infrastructure building in the form of new schools, parks, dams, port facilities, housing, hospitals, airports, public buildings, and streets and highways. These projects have several purposes: to get money flowing, provide jobs, stimulate future development, and reflect credit on the government initiating them. To visitors from countries with stagnant economies, the Dominican Republic seems vibrantly alive with dynamic construction projects.

The high level of public investment has also stimulated private investment. Data from 1978 show that funds from Dominican savings and loan associations used for new housing construction totaled $78 million, a high figure for so small a country. Dominican businessmen are also investing more in their own country instead of sending their profits to

The new Valdesia dam

Miami or Switzerland. Foreign investment, as we have seen, is also growing.

Public investment has not only resulted in the pumping of millions of dollars into the economy (over $300 million in 1978), but has also provided a gigantic boost to construction and subsidiary industries. Construction is now second only to mining as the major new growth area. In many respects public investment in construction is central to the whole modernization effort. Although economic well-being still depends heavily on sugar, mining, and tourism, construction is highly visible modernization. Building roads, dams, schools, and hospitals is not only good in itself, in both the short and the long term, but such construction projects are also symbols of growth, progress, and dynamism.

To ensure that these visible and tangible signs of development continue, the government embarked on an ambitious three-year plan in 1979 to spend $1.7 billion of public, private, and foreign funds to finance additional infrastructure building. Through such massive infusions of capital, the Dominicans hope to provide jobs immediately, and a base on which further economic development can be built.

Private foreign investment, especially in tourism, light industry, and mining, has also been encouraged. Moreover, there is now for the first time considerable coordination between the public and private spheres, and even some joint ventures. To attract new foreign investment, the government has taken the initiative to provide personal investment assistance from high-level officials, an expanded public relations campaign, tax exemption programs, and other incentives. Government institutions such as the Central Bank, the Corporation for Industrial Development, CEDOPEX, and the Ministry of Industry and Commerce, have all been utilized to assist potential investors to overcome complicated legal procedures and to file the registration applications required of any new company formed with foreign capital. Government officials have been actively assuring foreign investors of stability, security, and profitability. Interestingly, this effort to lure foreign capital carried over from the conservative, business-oriented regime of Balaguer to the social-democratic administration of Guzmán.

A major reason for the recent increase in foreign investment is the development of three industrial free zones in the country. Established in Santiago, La Romana, and San Pedro de Macorís, the zones were designed to attract foreign and local manufacturers. The industries enjoy tax exemptions (for up to twenty years), import incentives, export exemptions, and exemptions from minimum wage. Since their formation during the Balaguer government, forty-five firms have built factories in the three zones. Many are "platform industries", that is, industries where raw materials are brought in from abroad and finished products (clothing, industrial staples) are sold abroad; only the manufacturing is done in the Dominican Republic – but there is no uniform pattern. Corporate income from the free zones is estimated at $50 million.

While strenuously trying to attract foreign investment, the Dominicans have also been conscious of its dangers. Hence, Public Law 861 was enacted which outlines the foreign investment policy of the government. The law sets strict guidelines on which areas are open to foreign investment ("enterprises dedicated to the exportation of goods and services") and which ones are reserved for the state ("public services, mining, hydrocarbons, defense, forest exploitation, and domestic trade").

The most controversial section of the law is that concerning remittances of the profits from investment. The law allows foreign companies to remit or send back to corporate headquarters 18 percent of the profits from their Dominican-based enterprises. The law is unclear, however, as to how funds used for reinvestment affect profit calculations. Uncertainty over how the law will be interpreted has caused apprehension among foreign investors, and some reports indicate foreign investment is leveling off.

Criticism by foreign investors forced the government to order a re-evaluation of Public Law 861, and has spurred a reexamination of other laws pertaining to foreign investment. Public Law 146, passed in 1971 to regulate exploration and extraction of Dominican mineral resources, is also under reconsideration in order to (in the words of the government) "offer investors a more reliable and consistent legal framework, while allowing the Dominican state a more equitable share of the benefits derived from the exploitation of these nonrenewable resources."

The Dominican Republic remains an attractive place to invest, despite the recent discussion over Public Law 861. A 1980 visit by a mission from the Overseas Private Investment Corporation (OPIC), a quasi-official U.S. agency that assists foreign investors and insures them against loss, gave an added boost to private investment in its report. The mission, which included twenty-five business executives, concluded that "The government of the Dominican Republic is stable, progressive and has a strong commitment to private enterprise. The private sector is strong, innovative and aggressive, there is a large, trainable work force and impressive free trade zones already have been established. Finally the country is strategically located to serve the Caribbean and Latin-American markets."

Tourism

Tourism is another area in which the Dominican Republic hopes to achieve long-term economic success. Tourism, never important before, has now become a major industry. In 1971, 137,000 tourists visited the Dominican Republic; by 1978 the figure had risen to 460,000, with over 500,000 expected in subsequent years. The Dominican Republic is now being presented as "the land Columbus loved best" and "the best kept secret in the Caribbean."

Annual income derived from tourism is presently about $100 million. The benefits accruing from tourism, however, are more than increased revenue. Tourism also means jobs for thousands of impoverished Dominicans as baggage handlers, cab drivers, maids, waiters, grounds keepers, etc. These are often demeaning and not very high-paying jobs, but they are certainly better than no jobs at all.

Increased tourism also means increased air flights to the country, more construction (there are now some four thousand hotel rooms), and more government investment. To help service the new hotels, the government has constructed airports, built new roads and water systems, expanded electrical capacity, and modernized whole sections of cities—the "old city" in the center of Santo Domingo and the old port town of Puerto Plata on the north coast. To monitor the tourist projects undertaken with public funds, the government created another agency, INFRATUR, in 1971. INFRATUR has invested $76 million so far in tourism-related infrastructure projects, of which fully half was used to refurbish and spruce up Puerto Plata.

The Dominican government seems dedicated to expanding tourism and attracting the tourist dollar. The 1979 budget, for the first time, included a line item allocating $2.7 million for overseas promotion of the Dominican Republic. Under Balaguer, additionally, a Tourist Incentive Law was passed, which provided tax breaks and fee exemptions for investors in the tourist industry. Finally, President Guzmán elevated the head of tourism to a cabinet position.

The Dominicans are well aware of the limitations of tourism as a means of increasing national revenues. But while other Caribbean islands are household words in the tourist industry, the Dominican Republic is a fresh and virtually untouched paradise. The Dominican government is banking on the "discovery" of the country as a long-term bonanza that will generate millions of dollars in foreign currency while enabling them further to diversify their economy.

International Assistance

Dominicans increasingly feel they must control and direct their own development process, yet the government realizes that it must maintain a close working arrangement with the United States and the international lending agencies. In recent decades, the United States has been the major source of assistance and loans. Between 1946 and 1977 the United States provided the Dominican Republic with $520 million in economic assistance and an additional $144 million through the Food for Peace program, under Public Law 480. During the troubled years of the 1960s, the United States gave more aid per capita to the Dominican Republic than to any other country in the world.

In recent years, U.S. economic assistance has been greatly reduced and concentrated in a limited number of areas: agriculture, vocational training, highway maintenance, family planning, food and health care, and alternative energy development. Estimates for 1979 placed U.S. aid at $32.5 million, derived chiefly from three sources: the Agency for International Development (AID), Food for Peace, and the Commodity Credit Corporation.

The assistance programs of the United States in the Guzmán years came under attack in the Dominican Republic primarily because of the budget cuts of the Carter and Reagan administrations and the U.S. Congress. Much of the hurricane assistance promised by the United States has yet to materialize, and other aid dealing with energy planning and assistance is still tied up in the Congress. The Dominicans agree that as one of the few surviving democracies in Latin America, with an enviable human rights record, they deserve better. Although U.S. officials point with pride to nearly $120 million in aid to the Dominican Republic in the years 1977–1980, a large proportion of that money has not actually been delivered.

The failure of the United States to provide the promised development assistance has forced the Dominican Republic to negotiate other bilateral, multilateral, and private loan arrangements. A sugar-for-petroleum arrangement, for example, has been negotiated with oil-rich Venezuela. Spain recently approved a $60 million loan to finance construction of a thermoelectric plant to aid the Dominican Republic's growing demand for energy. West Germany has provided $14 million in hurricane relief, and Israel has provided technical assistance for the establishment of rural cooperatives in arid zones.

Although such bilateral assistance has been substantial and from diverse sources, the Dominican Republic has also felt compelled to approach international lending agencies for additional aid. The Inter-American Development Bank (IADB) has been the primary source. Through 1978 the IADB provided $306 million; in 1979 another $66 million was added. The loans have gone primarily for agricultural modernization, a high priority of the Guzmán administration. The World Bank has also been approached for loans: recently, $50 million was approved for a highway project and another $25 million to support imports.

Heavy reliance on borrowing from the international lending institutions has created a number of debt management problems. Currently the national debt is $1.4 billion. The government so far has met all its foreign debt payment requirements, but repayment has posed a budgetary problem and will continue to do so, especially if revenues from exports continue to drop. Fortunately for the Dominican government, the repayment schedules of the IADB and World Bank are not as harsh as those found in the private sector, and it is with the IADB that most of its loans have been contracted.

ECONOMIC EFFECTS OF NATURAL DISASTERS: THE HURRICANES

The aggressive efforts of Dominican authorities to modernize the country's economy, resolve its social problems, and lessen its dependency on external markets and funding were placed in severe jeopardy in 1979. Hurricane David and Tropical Storm Frederick both hit the island hard, causing over $1 billion in damages, killing 1,000 and leaving

400,000 homeless. These were not the first tropical storms to devastate the Dominican Republic, nor would they likely be the last. Hispaniola lies right in the path of the hurricanes that originate in the Atlantic before churning west and north, and periodically they wreak immense damage on the island.

The extent of the damage from the 1979 storms may be gleaned from the Dominican government's own report: "Electrical installations, telephone networks, highways, bridges, and factories were destroyed. Coffee production in the south-central area was almost entirely ruined; coconut and plantain crops were 75% destroyed; the poultry and livestock industry was virtually decimated. An overall assessment of the losses to the Dominican economy indicates the magnitude of the catastrophe: 16% of the gross national product, 80% of the total investment of a normal year, more than 120% of 1978 exports, and more than 140% of the government's current income."

The Dominican government earmarked $140 million for its recovery program and received substantial assistance from the United States and West Germany, the IADB, and private firms, such as Philip Morris. It began the repair of irrigation systems, roads, electrical facilities, housing and bridges; in nine months, some 75–80 percent of the repairs had been made. Yet, despite this remarkable recovery, the Dominican Republic has found its efforts to achieve economic growth and greater independence interrupted and set back.

Perhaps even more damaging than the physical destruction caused by the hurricane are the longer-term effects it had on the economy as a whole. The loss of the coffee and cocoa crops, the interruption in foreign investment, the setbacks to government housing and other programs, and the decline in gross domestic product, all translate into diminished national revenues, greater balance of payments deficits, runaway inflation, additional foreign debt, the need for more imports, higher unemployment, lower living standards, and seriously heightened social pressures among the lower classes. The 1979 storms not only wreaked havoc, but reinforced the viewpoint, deeply ingrained in the Dominicans, that despite all their efforts to build the nation and strengthen the economy, they remain destined always to be set back— that they are vulnerable to circumstances, man-made and natural, that are completely out of their control.

THE FUTURE OF THE DOMINICAN ECONOMY

Speculating on any nation's future economic development is risky. This is especially so in the Dominican case, with its history of political ups and downs and an economy subject to unpredictable and uncontrollable external forces. Caution and balance are required.

Few in the Dominican Republic now think that the country can again match its "miracle" growth rates of the early-to-mid-1970s; oil price increases and the depressed state of commodity prices largely rule that out. Yet, the Dominican economy and people have shown a remarkable resistance to adversity. Despite their continued existence as a small and dependent nation, despite natural calamity, and despite immense social and economic problems, the Dominican economy is showing renewed vitality. Agricultural production increased in 1980, foreign investment continues to flow in, imports have leveled off, tourism is booming, and the economy is less and less dependent on King Sugar.

Looking at the price of petroleum, the high unemployment, the balance of payments deficits, and the structural weaknesses in the economy, a pessimistic outlook on the economic future of the Dominican Republic is understandable. Yet Dominicans remain optimistic, seeing these problems as solvable rather than permanent obstacles to modernization and development. Much of the optimism stems from the sense of stability and confidence that Presidents Balaguer and Guzmán carried with them into the National Palace.

Guzmán offered a mix of humane social programs with some hard-nosed and realistic economic modernization plans. A social-democrat, he had also been a businessman and landowner; he was certainly no wide-eyed radical bent on soaking the rich, throwing out the Americans, or expropriating property. That, of course, made him unacceptable to the left, including some within his own party who denounced him as a "bourgeois landowner" and a "transitional figure," but it made him acceptable to the business-commercial community, where real power in the Dominican Republic lies. Guzmán sought to persuade all groups that hard work, cooperation, and patience will pay off in terms of both a brighter economic future and more just social programs.

Guzmán's success in creating a climate for continued growth, while also preserving democracy and human rights, was in large part due to his conducting government business in a different manner from his predecessor. He refused to make secret deals with the big foreign firms, he cut out corruption in high places, he delivered real substantive programs rather than public relations campaigns, and he sought a proper and prudent balance between the necessities of economic growth and the requirements of social justice. Guzmán pledged to attain economic development in a context of honesty, compassion, fairness, and democracy.

As in much of the Third World, the Dominican Republic must walk a tightrope. The margin for error is small; disaster looms if the tightrope walker loses balance. Yet in the Dominican case one cannot help but be impressed by the mood of confidence and determination, by the commitment to democracy, by the assurance, even after so many setbacks, that the nation will in fact achieve economic modernization, some measure of independence, and that place in the sun to which it has always aspired.

7

Political Institutions and Processes

If the economy is the lifeblood of the Dominican Republic, then politics can be viewed as its "soul," the very essence of what is Dominican. Both must be cared for and nourished for survival. The Dominican people today clearly understand the influence that sugar prices, inflation, and international markets have on their national life; but it is politics, leadership, the contest for national power that fires their imagination, calls them to action, and defines their world.

Politics in the Dominican Republic is serious business. It is more than a mechanical process of placing people in office to make routine decisions. To the Dominicans politics provides a forum where the most basic issues of national life are debated and often fought over. Politics is not a campaign merely of competing programs and public relations efforts, but a life-and-death struggle to establish certain principles or obtain a preferred and advantageous system of governance. The stakes are high: immense power, position, and status for those who achieve the presidency or ride the president's coattails into office; opportunities for jobs, sinecures, and private enrichment that go with high office; and the prestige and strength that accompany capture of the very pinnacles of the Dominican system. Because the stakes are high, the competition is fierce and frequently violent. Unlike many of the advanced industrial democracies, where alternations in power are routinely accepted and cause little discord, the Dominican Republic continues to reveal deep-seated disagreements over the shape and direction of politics and government administration.

THE TENSION OF COMPETING POLITICAL PHILOSOPHIES

At the heart of Dominican politics lies the conflict between those who believe the country must be governed by an authoritarian and elite-

91

dominated system and those who believe in greater freedom and democracy.

Like many of its sister republics in Latin America, the Dominican political system derived substantially from the Spanish system of centralized authority, hierarchy, order, discipline, and rule from the top down. These traditions have been reinforced by the Dominicans' own history of disorder, revolt, underdevelopment, repeated foreign invasions, and lack of strong institutions. It is argued that only authoritarian rule, iron-clad discipline, and government emanating from the top down, not from the bottom up, can secure the order and stability necessary for development, preventing chaos, repelling foreign threats, and holding together a country that tends toward fragmentation and breakdown.

Authoritarianism went virtually unchallenged during the three centuries of Spanish domination and the ensuing decades of Haitian control. But when the Dominicans gained their independence in 1844, liberalism and republicanism became the ideals. The liberal tenets included limited government, human rights, and free elections.

The competition between the authoritarian and the liberal currents formed the backdrop for much of the Dominican conflict in the nineteenth and twentieth centuries. The liberal Duarte was replaced by the twin authoritarians, Báez and Santana. The next short-lived liberal regime led to the dictatorship of Heureaux. The chaos and anarchy that followed his assassination led first to a U.S. Marine occupation, and then to Trujillo.

The Trujillo regime carried the authoritarian tradition to its extreme: full-fledged totalitarianism. Heureaux and Trujillo also came closest to resurrecting the still-venerated sixteenth-century Spanish model of a centralized unitary regime, though both went too far and were eventually killed for their excesses. Both sought to eliminate the competing liberal current.

With Trujillo's death in 1961, the competition between these two philosophies of governance was renewed with vigor. The Dominican Republic became a major battleground between liberals and liberalism's skeptics. The chronology is familiar: first a conservative Council of State; then the liberal regime of Juan Bosch, which was promptly overthrown; back to conservative rule; then the revolution, civil war, and American intervention of 1965; again, conservative rule under Balaguer; and liberal rule once more under Guzmán.

Over the years, the authoritarian tradition in the Dominican Republic has been gradually weakened and the liberal one slowly strengthened. Yet it would be inaccurate to say the Dominicans have reached a consensus on their political system. There is still too much

Ex-President Joaquín Balaguer (at microphone) and the powers behind the throne (1966)

disagreement over ultimate goals to make such a judgment. The liberal current seems to be gaining, but it could be snuffed out again quite easily.

Two additional points deserve mention. The first has to do with the values of the younger generation now coming to power and of a larger and more affluent middle class, and whether these signal a long-term strengthening of the liberal tradition. We do not know what the precise implications of these changes will be, but we do know the younger generation is often more liberal and open to new ideas than their more authoritarian elders, and that sizable portions of the emerging middle class have a strong interest in both stability and democracy. At some time in the future, however, the middle-class values of stability and democracy are likely to prove incompatible, and Dominicans will have to choose between them.

The other point is that a third current, socialism, is growing in the Dominican Republic in competition with the other two. Future Dominican politics will involve conflict between all three currents: conservative-authoritarian, liberal-democratic, and socialist. Hence, while the Dominican Republic may have begun to resolve some of its earlier conflicts, it now faces the prospect of having still another viewpoint and source of conflict come to the fore.

THE RULES OF THE GAME

The heritage of disagreement, struggle, and conflict that has so strongly dominated Dominican politics has helped foster a set of operating rules and requirements for participation, leadership, and policy making. A central tenet has been that politics is a "zero-sum game." The total social and economic product has historically been more or less fixed, so that if one person or group wins, another must lose. Dominican politics is thus a winner-take-all proposition in which virtually any tactics may be used to get to power and stay there.

This implies that a government in power usually treats its opponents as traitors, while the opposition usually views the government as, at best, usurpers. Opposition groups must practice the politics of patient survival, often from exile, for the government often uses repression and intimidation against them. To be an oppositionist requires perseverance, bravery, and ingenuity. The proposition that governs the relations between government and opposition is usually: "Winner takes all, loser takes survival."

Dominican history contains numerous examples of these prevailing patterns. Most often, it has been the advocates of authoritarian rule who have "taken all" and it has been the democrats who have been forced to take "survival." Although such "out" groups as the PRD are more democratically inclined and willing to allow opposition freedom, when in office the PRD has not shown much propensity to involve the opposition in decision making or to share with it the spoils of power. The view that the winner monopolizes the administration and that the opposition languishes in oblivion remains firmly entrenched.

There are some who argue that this is now changing. Whether it is a long-term change in the pattern of politics, or is only a short-term phenomenon caused by the expanding economic pie that presently has more pieces to hand out to more groups, cannot now be ascertained. However, there is no doubt that under President Guzmán some major new initiatives were taken.

The first major change concerned the legislature and legislative-executive relations. Under an arrangement worked out when Guzmán's election hung in the balance, the PRD agreed to an allocation of seats in the Dominican Congress that gave Balaguer's Reformista Party control of the Senate. The PRD controled the Chamber of Deputies, but the Senate is viewed as the more prestigious body, and has some special powers of judicial appointment which could conceivably affect a presidential succession.

As a result of this arrangement, and perhaps for the first time in Dominican history, a strong and viable opposition emerged in the Congress, which under Guzmán was allowed to make its voice heard. Under Balaguer, the PRD opposition had been largely silenced, but under Guzmán, executive-legislative relations were lively. The legislative sessions were marked by vigorous debate and considerable legislative action in such areas as land reform, human rights, disaster relief, and the role of multinationals in Dominican national life. The legislature became not an equal of the executive branch, but it gained influence as a forum for debate on public policy, and certainly that a strong opposition voice was allowed at all represents a major change.

The second major innovation involves the broad-based team of advisors that Guzmán appointed. Although he received severe criticism for appointing his daughter and other relatives and friends to key government posts (old traditions die hard!), Guzmán also brought into his administration persons from all sectors of Dominican society: PRDistas, Balagueristas, conservative businessmen, leftist reformers, technicians, and military officers. The criteria used for appointment in most cases were merit and experience, not special connections. Indeed, some of the harshest criticism of Guzmán came from his own party members who felt they had not received an adequate share of the government jobs. Guzmán also moved to attract higher quality people to government (and simultaneously eliminate the temptations for illegal enrichment) by raising the salaries of ministers and other high officials.

The third change initiated by Guzmán involved his effort to create a

President Antonio Guzmán in February 1979

government of national unity and reconciliation. Unlike his pre-decessors, whose policies often divided and polarized society, Guzmán sought to lessen tensions between traditional enemies. The President generally spoke softly, sought balance, and governed with dignity. Political exiles of the left and right were allowed to return home, wages were raised while the fears of businessmen were assuaged, the military leaders were sought out for advice, and the rural and urban poor were promised new programs to address past inequities. Guzmán sought unity and pragmatism as a means to achieve the development that all Dominicans desire.

Guzmán achieved some notable successes in his efforts to heal old wounds and to command the moderate left and center of the political spectrum. Disgruntled factions remained, but under Guzmán the coun-try was unified as never before. Old enemies from the 1965 civil war returned to the country and were again on speaking terms; a positive and optimistic mood developed as many of the old hatreds were put aside. This lessening of ancient animosities was one of the major ac-complishments of the past few years.

Of course, it all depends on the economic pie. If it continues to ex-pand, and more and more people get access to the pieces, then the an-cient "zero-sum" nature of the Dominican political game will have undergone a major transformation. But should the pie stop expanding or actually shrink, then the old habits and tensions are likely to surface again.

THE CHARACTER OF LEADERSHIP

The discussion above not only emphasizes the significant contribu-tions of Guzmán but also points to the importance of presidential leader-ship in Dominican politics. The president (any president) is the hub and center of the system. If he does well, the country will likely thrive; if he is a disaster, the country can as easily slide down hill. The president has a responsibility, in a personal sense, for both the direction of the collec-tive national life and the well-being of individual citizens.

Dominican politics rests almost exclusively on the quality of per-sonal presidential leadership. From the time of Duarte, the "dual caudillos," and Heureaux through Trujillo, Bosch, Balaguer, and Guzmán, the country has been shaped not so much by formal constitu-tional and institutional arrangements, but rather by the talents, *per-sonalismo*, charisma, strength, and machismo of the individuals who oc-cupied the National Palace.

The Dominican political system, as in other countries of Latin

America, is organized in highly personalistic terms, and its processes of policy making are seen as the direct responsibility of the president. But while government in most of the other Latin American countries has become increasingly bureaucratic and institutionalized in recent decades, that has happened far less in the Dominican Republic. The president makes all decisions, passes on all appointments, holds all the reins in his hands. He is not only the central figure in the hierarchy, he is also largely alone. The president formulates proposals, introduces them to the people, sees that they are enacted, monitors their implementation, and, of course, claims all credit for their success.

The centrality and singularity of executive leadership implies a set of personal qualities necessary for effective management of the government and survival in an often hostile and competitive environment. The Dominican leaders who may have had the most influence on the shape and direction of the country—Heureaux, Trujillo, Balaguer—all possessed similar leadership characteristics. All three governed as authoritarians and sought to present themselves as builders and modernizers, as men who provided unity and constructive progress in a nation that had previously been divided and lacked development. Despite the fact that in all three cases development projects were limited largely to infrastructure building rather than providing more basic human services, these leaders were masters of public relations, and effectively presented themselves as strong presidents of a nation on the move.

The sense of movement and dynamism generated by Heureaux, Trujillo, and Balaguer was linked to the use of repression against those who criticized them or their policies. They viewed their own power as supreme and uncontestable; those who challenged that premise were viewed as enemies and treated as such.

The outside observer might marvel at the resilience and longevity of the three presidents (Heureaux was in power seventeen years, Trujillo thirty-one, Balaguer twelve). The reason for their long terms in office cannot be ascribed simply to repression. All three presidents were not only shrewd manipulators, but they also presented themselves as paternalistic benefactors, providers of various goods and services, and national guardians who could garner public support even while ruling in an autocratic and often bloody fashion.

Ruling as manipulators, authoritarians, providers, and guardians, all three also presented themselves as benevolent father figures. In varying degrees and with varying styles, they seemed willing to listen to all citizen complaints and to resolve even the most trivial problems. This was done on a highly personal and individual basis; *organized* opposition or complaints were not permitted. Although all three were eventually revealed as power-hungry, self-serving tyrants, there is no doubt their rule was based on more than merely a police-state apparatus. Each of them retained his popularity for a long period. Hence, to many aspiring Dominican politicians, the Heureaux-Trujillo-Balaguer "model" remains attractive.

Authoritarian leadership in the Dominican Republic seems to require a talent for public relations, a willingness to use force, and a knack for paternalistic control. But it is essential to recognize that some Dominican presidents have viewed their roles and practiced a presidential style quite different from that pattern. Ulises Espaillat, Ramón Cáceres, Juan Bosch, and Antonio Guzmán stand out as leaders who were committed to the principles of democratic rule and who utilized democratic precepts as the basis for government.

Because of the different time periods in which they ruled and the changing social bases of their power, generalizations about these democratic presidents is difficult, yet it is possible to distinguish them rather sharply from the authoritarians. These rulers entered office as political reformers. All were determined to change the system. All encouraged reform and greater participation, and they were committed to respect for basic freedoms and democratic politics. All repudiated their autocratic predecessors. They all had visions of changing the political and economic order and the moral and ethical bases of Dominican society.

Their short terms in office, as compared with the authoritarians, have led many Dominicans to dismiss these brief experiments with democracy in the Dominican Republic as failures. Yet, it cannot be ignored that while they ruled, human rights were respected, democratic freedoms prevailed, reforms were carried out, and the democratic presidents themselves enjoyed widespread support. The accomplishments of the democratic leaders have been limited, but they should not be belittled, and much evidence indicates that the democratic tradition in the Dominican Republic remains very much alive.

This comparison of the authoritarians and the democrats in Dominican history leads us ultimately to consider the presidency of Antonio Guzmán. Guzmán was elected democratically and could hardly be considered an authoritarian. He compiled an enviable human rights record that is widely cited throughout the Americas, and he was also a social-democratic reformer.

But Guzmán developed a popularity transcending the usual party lines. Part of his popularity may be attributed to his ability to blend and reconcile both models of Dominican leadership. A democrat, he also pursued a more traditional leadership style. He presented himself not as a

radical reformer, but as a nation builder, a modernizer, an adroit or-
chestrator of economic development. He travelled a moderate course,
seeking not to antagonize any major group, but to preside over a government of national unity. His ability and willingness to compromise meant
that, unlike the older tyrants, he was able to avoid the excessive use of
force, though he did not hesitate to assert his leadership when that was
called for.

The leadership style of Guzmán, which combined the two dominant traditions in Dominican history, is not an easy one to maintain. It
requires the ability to reconcile conflicting objectives and modes of
operation that are poles apart. Guzmán was successful in maintaining
this balancing act during his administration, but it is impossible to speak
with great confidence about the future. If a new synthesis has been
achieved, it can only bode well for Dominican stability and development. But if the Guzmán presidency proves to be only a temporary in-
terlude, then the political system may be expected to revert to the more
"normal" tension and oscillation between authoritarian and democratic
rule.

THE CONTEST FOR POWER

Although politics in the Dominican Republic is often shaped and
defined by competition between rival "men-on-horseback" and their
retinues, rival personalities and governing styles, and rival philosophical
traditions, the system is more complex than that. Politics also takes the
form of "ins" versus "outs," (blues versus reds, as they were called
historically), factional fights and quarrels, and, above all, wholly different conceptions on the part of distinct groups, pertaining to quite different historical epochs and life styles, as to the proper shape and direction of the national life.

Since the 1960s, the "in" group has been a coalition of conservative
interests led by Joaquín Balaguer, while the "out" group consisted of a
more ill-defined coalition of liberal-democratic or social-democratic interests led by Juan Bosch (until he resigned and formed his own party)
and the Dominican Revolutionary Party. To some, this contest has been
reduced to a simpler contest between two rival modern-day caudillos,
Bosch and Balaguer; but in reality the division goes deeper than that. It
involves a contest between two rival "families," one conservative and
traditional in its political preferences and the other modern and change-
oriented. This basic split lies at the heart of Dominican politics and helps
account for its tensions, conflict, and frequent resorts to violence.

The players in this contest have not changed substantially since the assassination of Trujillo. On the one side are the major landowners, business interests, military officers, high Church officials, some elements of the emerging middle class, and usually the U.S. embassy. These are the more conservative or status quo–oriented elements, or those who favor change but only within the parameters of the existing system. They are led, as they have been generally since the early 1960s, by Joaquín Balaguer. Balaguer successfully separated his support and leadership style from that of Trujillo, offering a somewhat more tolerant attitude toward dissent and organized opposition while continuing to rule in an authoritarian and conservative fashion. This group represents what might be called the "family of order."

Balaguer's supporters never developed a cohesive or ideologically well-defined party organization. For elective purposes and to give the outside world (especially the United States) the impression of an emerging party system in the Dominican Republic, they formed the Partido Reformista, or Reformist Party. But this party consisted chiefly of the personal followers and retinue of Balaguer, and had no real programmatic or ideological basis. It served as the reelection vehicle for Balaguer and as a giant national patronage and spoils agency, but it never developed as a modern political party organization.

Balaguer did not need a strong party organization to bolster his presidency or ensure his reelection. He presented himself and his regime as "traditionally Dominican," above partisan politics, a national unity movement rather than divisively party-based. Balaguer was a more modern caudillo who, though supported by the same coalition of interests as Trujillo had been, proved that conservative objectives could be realized without resort to extensive and brutal repression.

Whereas Balaguer represented the "ins" and the forces for the status quo, the PRD, Bosch, and more recently Guzmán sought to speak for the "outs," the traditionally forgotten elements in Dominican society.

The PRD represents the forces for change. It has been molded as a more modern political party with a definite program and ideology. Founded by Bosch as an exile organization, it led much of the opposition to the Trujillo regime. The party is committed to democracy and social reform. It represents the antithesis of the older tradition of conservatism and authoritarianism. Its followers come from the ranks of the urban working class, the aroused and aware peasantry, young professionals and students, some sectors of the middle class, and some elements within the military and clergy.

We have analyzed the failure of the PRD to achieve its stated goals in 1963, 1965, and throughout the repressive Balaguer era; equally significant have been the internal divisions within the party during this period. The PRD has been plagued by almost continuous factional disputes concerning the advisability of its continued commitment to liberal democracy, the most effective opposition tactics, and the role of leadership within the party. These splits have drained the party of some of its key leaders and, at times, led to bitter wrangling. The disputes over leadership and ideology eventually precipitated the departure of Bosch in 1973, and he formed a rival, presumably more revolutionary organization, called the Party of Dominican Liberation (PLD).

Bosch's departure, however, did not quiet the internal friction between the more left-wing socialists within the party and its more moderate social-democrats. Juan Francisco Peña Gómez, a Bosch protégé, rose to the position of party secretary-general and continued to urge a shift to the left. Peña Gómez has called for the nationalization of Gulf and Western, and for Dominican recognition of Communist Cuba.

The more leftist-nationalist views of Peña Gómez are counterbalanced by the moderate and conciliatory element led by Antonio Guzmán. Guzmán represents a less strident, less confrontational, and less ideological posture, which is also held by most elder statesmen within the party who still hold firmly to the ideals of liberal democracy and consensus politics.

In order to achieve electoral victory in 1978, Peña Gómez and Guzmán joined ranks and presented a united front, but after Guzmán took power the rift between the two party leaders widened. What began as polite criticism of each other's position on occasion turned into open hostility. Peña Gómez lamented the inadequate social programs of the government and urged faster and more vigorous redistribution efforts. He denounced his own president and party head as a bourgeois landowner and purely transitional figure. Guzmán responded by reminding the secretary-general of the need for pragmatism, give-and-take, and the difficulties of democratic rule in a country as volatile as the Dominican Republic.

The conflict between Peña Gómez and Guzmán weakened the PRD's hopes of retaining control of the government. Although the potential for even more serious disputes is real, both sides also recognized the need to cooperate. In 1979, when urban rioting broke out after the announcement of major gasoline price increases, President Guzmán felt compelled to ask Peña Gómez to quiet the crowd. Without the pleading of the popular and charismatic Peña, the riot could have become even more serious and threatened Guzmán's power base. The fact that Guzmán made the decision, but had to ask Peña to put out the fire, not only points clearly to the realities of power in the Dominican Republic, but also indicates the need of the PRD leadership to work together if democracy is to survive.

The struggle between the "family of order" and the "family of change" is probably the major arena of Dominican politics, but there are other political actors as well. The Revolutionary Social Christian Party, now rebaptized as the Social Action Christian Movement, is thought by many to be the third most important party in the country. In the past, the Christian-democrats have often been aligned with the PRD, but when Guzmán became president they became vocal critics of the government.

Another group with some support is the Partido Quisqueyano Dominicano (PQD). The PQD is the personal apparatus of former General Elías Wessin y Wessin, who led the conservative forces in the 1965 civil war. Both right-wing and populist, the PQD lingers on the political scene, but it is based on the dwindling personal following of Wessin and has no real program or ideology.

The most vocal and active of the smaller groups is the Dominican Communist Party (PCD). Led by Narcisio Isa Conde, this party was only recently declared legal. It has a small cadre of student leaders and young professionals, but has not attracted much popular support. It criticizes the government for the slowness of its reforms, but its visibility in the form of wall posters and painted slogans is considerably greater than its actual strength.

The catalog of political parties could go on with mention of a number of purely personalistic and small splinter groups that usually surface around election time and disappear shortly thereafter. These parties add color and complexity to the political scene, but their influence is weak and their staying power negligible.

Overall, it is hard to say that a strong and well-institutionalized political party system has been established in the Dominican Republic. The Partido Reformista is likely to split up once Balaguer passes out of politics, but we have seen that conservative and business groups have other means of making their influences felt. With the exception of the Social-Christians and the Communists, the minor parties have not been prone to last. Only on the left, in the PRD, is there a strong and viable political party, and even that has been torn by divisiveness.

THE DECISIONMAKING PROCESS

In most Western democratic systems, the structures of government and the procedures for formulating and implementing public policies are understood to be at the center of national politics. Policy decisions made in this context emerge as a result of complex and often cumbersome bargaining among elected politicians, appointed bureaucrats, strong interest groups, and an articulated public opinion. The slow and difficult process by which policy is determined in such systems is viewed as a necessary evil inherent in the participatory decisionmaking, the constitutionally defined procedures, and the cautious, incremental approach of democratic decisionmaking.

The Dominican structure and process of decisionmaking has not, historically, always conformed to this Western and democratic tradition. Rather, it combines a great deal of elaborate form with some questionable substance. The Dominican constitutional tradition has long reflected the forms of the U.S. Constitution. In the heyday of Dominican caudilloism one could always find lavishly detailed constitutions, long lists of human rights, the tripartite separation of powers, festive presidential elections, and power formally defined as emanating from the bottom up. These forms were obviously quite different from the operating realities.

Even in modern times this gap between constitutional formalities and the actual substance of politics persists. The formal separation of powers barely disguises an imperial presidency, local government is weak or nonexistent, elections may be rigged or used to ratify a president already in power rather than providing for genuine choice. Instead of reflecting a diversity of independent institutions and interests involved in an open and competitive policy process, Dominican decisionmaking often remains a closed system in which the president and a handful of cronies can determine policies, without much consultation and with little respect for public opinion or democratic procedures.

The present-day Dominican political system is still modeled closely after that of the United States. A constitution promulgated in 1966 by the Balaguer government provides its legal basis. The constitution provides for the familiar three-part division of powers and a bicameral legislature (a Senate of twenty-seven members and a Chamber of Deputies of ninety-one). The country is organized into twenty-six provinces plus the National District (Santo Domingo). The constitution also contains a detailed bill of rights.

There are many similarities in this constitution, at the formal level, to that of the United States. But the underlying political realities are often quite distinct. During Balaguer's rule the presidency was the overwhelmingly dominant institution. The legislative and judicial branches were decidedly subordinate. Human rights were routinely violated.

In order to publicize and implement his programs effectively, Balaguer counted on a coalition of loyal government bureaucrats, Reformista Party officials, military and police enforcers, political cronies, and the provincial governors (all of whom were women). Seldom was public policy the subject of open parliamentary debate, let alone of judicial scrutiny. Rather, Balaguer consulted quietly with friends, planners, and economists in the Ministries of Finance and Industry and Commerce, and in the Central Bank. Policy decisions were promulgated as decree-laws.

The failure of Balaguer's regime to translate the formalities of the constitutional framework into real and functioning democratic political practices is best illustrated by the human rights situation during his presidency. Despite clear constitutional provisions for the protection of civil liberties, the Balaguer regime was unwilling to establish the rule of law in the country. Besides Balaguer's feeble and half-hearted efforts to bring police, military, and paramilitary terror under control, the silence of the legislature, the courts, and national officials, in the face of widespread violations of human rights, showed that the formal constitutional system was largely inoperative – a facade. The activities of the so-called uncontrollable forces (secret police and military units) raised questions as to whether President Balaguer was actually running the government, or if these other groups were.

The pattern of systematic constitutional neglect fostered by Balaguer and many of his predecessors does not die easily. The habits of executive predominance regardless of what the constitution says, of systematic and purposeful violations of human rights, and of illegal military and police activities, are deeply ingrained in the Dominican political culture. Yet the Guzmán administration inaugurated in 1978 brought some notable changes to the way the system works.

Guzmán, like Balaguer, perhaps like all Dominican presidents, governed in a highly imperious and personal fashion, at times with little concern for the other branches of government. Guzmán also relied on a small coterie of friends and advisers in the formulation of policy. The differences can be found, however, in the increasing importance of and attention to legislative debate, the institution of a government of laws, respect for human rights, and a tolerance of diversity, even though those tolerated often attack the government itself.

Perhaps the best illustration of this commitment to constitutionality and democratic government is in the area of human rights. A study done by the U.S. Congress and supported by independent reports from Amnesty International, provides ample evidence for the changes ushered in by the Guzmán administration. In 1978, the new government released 200 political prisoners and brought some needed reforms to the infamous prison, La Victoria. The government also enacted a liberal amnesty law enabling scores of exiles to return home. These changes, plus greater opportunities for opposition groups to organize, demonstrate, and disseminate literature, earned the Guzmán administration high marks. The Dominican Republic was among the freest and most democratic countries in Latin America.

The changes in the policy-making process and in the functioning of the entire governmental system under Guzmán brought new life and hope to the Dominican Republic. A new sense of national pride became evident. The country ranked right up there with Costa Rica and Venezuela on the major indexes of democracy and human rights. It provided a model of how to shift from authoritarian to democratic rule.

But one needs to step back from this talk of fundamental transformation, of the Dominican "success story," to ask just how basic the changes have been and whether they will be lasting. We must recognize that the processes of social, economic, and political development have been, and will continue to be, long, arduous, and erratic. There are no quick fixes, no easy solutions. While Guzmán and the PRD moved to inculcate the spirit of democracy, to foster healthy political discussion and diversity, and to reestablish the rule of law, it must be remembered that these changes were new and not completely institutionalized. In all of Dominican history, after all, there have been only eight or ten years of democratic government, and the interim between the last attempt and Guzmán's was fully fifteen years. Democratic rule is not a system of governance with which the Dominicans have had long experience. Caution is therefore essential when analyzing the current state and future directions of Dominican politics.

What can be said with certainty is that Guzmán was more successful than Bosch in implementing liberal-democratic government in the Dominican Republic. The labyrinth of conflicting philosophies, allegiances, and interests analyzed here, which is fundamental to an understanding of the Dominican political system, also holds the key to the country's future as a democratic system.

8

Public Policy and Policymaking

Politics in the Dominican Republic is often defined in one-dimensional terms as an unrelenting quest for power and the privileges that accrue from it, or as an effort by those who have power and privileges to hang on to them at all costs and by those who don't to use whatever means are available to gain some for themselves. That is not an entirely inaccurate portrayal of Dominican politics – at least historically, and to a large extent even presently. But Dominican politics have become considerably more complex than the sheer struggle for power.

Once in office, political leaders must now face a wide range of problems and public policy issues that require them to make policy decisions on the allocation of scarce resources, the administration of government programs, and the proper direction of national development efforts. Dominican administrations must now rule not just for themselves, but also to satisfy popular demands for jobs, housing, water, education, economic development, and social programs of all sorts.

The attention given the problem of power and who controls it has obscured the growing importance of public policy in the Dominican Republic. In the modern era, particularly since Trujillo's death, Dominican politics have matured into a more complex process involving not just a struggle for power, but also the provision of government services in a wide range of areas. In short, public policy formulation and implementation has joined (but not superceded) the quest for power and privilege as an essential aspect of Dominican politics.

THE PUBLIC POLICY ENVIRONMENT

The formulation, enactment, and administration of public policy in the Dominican Republic, as elsewhere, is influenced by a unique configuration of social, political, and economic circumstances. In the

107

Dominican Republic, the circumstances in which public policy programs are carried out are well known: widespread poverty, economic dependency, vast social and economic gaps between the several classes, political instability and uncertainty, and intense – and rising – pressures for changes. Together, these and other factors have created formidable barriers to the effective development of public policy programs.

In this policy context, Dominican leaders have been forced to manage and manipulate a variety of domestic and foreign pressures when setting national priorities. A diversity of social and interest groups, economic forces, family alliances, and political party pressures must be satisfied if a policy is to succeed. Frequently, the enactment of a policy must be accompanied by payoffs, patronage, and other favors to disgruntled groups and individuals. Policy programs that serve a genuinely *public* interest are often lost in the effort to satisfy these private demands. And, of course, in a "zero-sum" society like the Dominican Republic, if one group gains from such policy measures, another is bound to lose and start plotting against the government.

In this as in other areas, the president remains the focus of the system. He still makes most major public policy decisions and must orchestrate the process of policy implementation. But by this time in the Dominican Republic there has also developed a large bureaucratic-administrative system. This includes the ministries and a whole range of special agencies and offices for the management of various national programs: agrarian reform, water resources, economic development, etc. In addition, the Dominican Republic has a comparatively large industrial sector that is government-owned, consisting chiefly of the former Trujillo businesses that were "inherited" by the government after the Trujillo family fled the country. Hence, while the Dominican public policy process remains president-centered, it has also become a much larger, more complex, and bureaucratized system with all the possibilities for graft, mismanagement, and ineffectiveness that that implies.

AGRICULTURAL VERSUS INDUSTRIAL DEVELOPMENT

One of the most fundamental arguments in the Dominican Republic is whether to assign priority to agricultural or to industrial development. It remains largely a rural, agricultural society with age-old traditions of working the land and the characteristic two-class social patterns of an agrarian society. Industrialization began under Trujillo, and its acceleration in recent decades, coupled with declining prices over a long term for commodities like sugar, have called into question the advisability of relying too heavily on agriculture. Primarily because of the price fluctuations for agricultural commodities, Dominican leaders have become convinced that diversification of the economy is essential for continued, stable growth.

Under Balaguer, the move toward diversification and industrialization began in earnest. The government moved forward with programs to lure foreign investment, build light industrial centers, explore for minerals, and shift public resources to heavy construction, transportation, and communications. During Balaguer's presidency, new port facilities were built, new leather and garment industries were established, and a variety of other factories began functioning. When Balaguer did shift his attention from industrialization to agriculture, it was usually in the form of grandiose dam building and irrigation projects that benefited large landowners and left small farmers without sorely needed farm machinery, fertilizer, or more modern farming techniques.

The emphasis on industrial development under Balaguer undoubtedly speeded up modernization, but it also created numerous social and economic problems that are still being felt today. One by-product was the massive influx of peasants into the cities because agriculture was languishing and there were no incentives to keep small farmers on the land. Massive urban migration has not only contributed further to the decline of agriculture, it has also created immense housing, sanitation, water, electricity, and other shortages in the cities. The daily arrival of hundreds of new city-dwellers has also placed added pressures on an already strained employment market.

Gulf and Western docks at La Romana

Perhaps the most serious problem of the emphasis on industrialization was the failure of agricultural production to keep pace with domestic demand. The country was obliged to import such basic foodstuffs as rice and beans. This revealed the neglect and decline of the agricultural sector, and forced the government to use scarce financial reserves to feed its own people.

The Guzman administration came into office with a quite different attitude. Perhaps because of his own farming background or his ideological sympathy for the plight of the peasant, Guzmán sought to redress the imbalance between agricultural and industrial development. He designated 1980 as the "year of agriculture" and moved forward on a number of fronts to rejuvenate the agricultural sector.

Primary emphasis was placed on irrigation, to benefit small farmers as well as large. Although Balaguer had begun some large irrigation projects, he had not provided the complementary facilities to make mechanized watering systems available. Using funds from the IADB, Guzmán sought to provide these facilities for rural irrigation.

Guzmán also expanded the program of rural credit. Coordinating such agencies as the Agricultural Bank, the Institute for Cooperative Development and Credit (IDECOOP), and the Office of Community Development (ODC), government officials began to provide more financing for small farmers.

The third facet of the government's agricultural policy was price stabilization. The Price Stabilization Institute (INESPRE), formed by Balaguer, is charged with using government funds to purchase domestic agricultural products and thereby ensure growers of a ready market at stable prices. In 1979, under Guzmán, INESPRE invested $10 million in direct purchases from producers. It also entered the foreign importation market to purchase agricultural products. Such importation arrangements, which amounted to $63 million in 1979, are designed to supplement domestic agricultural production in a way that does not jeopardize internal production or depress the fragile pricing mechanism.

The most controversial aspect of agricultural policy is land resettlement. The Guzmán administration pledged a more vigorous program to provide landless peasants with clear titles. In 1979, the government resettled close to a thousand families and distributed to them 137,809 *tareas* (21.5 thousand acres) of land. The government is proud of these agrarian reform efforts, but leftist critics view them as insufficient. The agrarian reform involved the doling out of land already in state hands, not nationalizations. Guzmán took a strong stand against the forcible seizure of private lands by peasants; on a number of occasions he reminded peasants, who constitute a major part of the government's base of support, that such seizures were illegal and would be met with swift judicial action.

The resettlement program faced major problems. The Dominican Agrarian Institute (IAD), which manages the program, underwent a number of leadership shakeups and was a focal point of criticism from the government's own party leaders. The PRD leaders were disenchanted with what they feel was an unfulfilled pledge by Guzmán to carry out extensive agrarian reform.

The renewed emphasis by Guzmán on agriculture did not shake what is now a continuing commitment to industrialization and diversification. New manufacturing plants continue to be encouraged and the desire to entice further foreign investment in the industrial sector remains, although with a firmer resolve to achieve more favorable contractual arrangements for the nation.

Manufacturing now accounts for 10 percent of gross domestic product and has a dollar value of $491.3 million, and much government effort has been directed toward ensuring this sector's continued growth. The government has formed a number of agencies designed to assist in financing, developing, and staffing new industrial enterprises. The Investment Fund for Economic Development (FIDE) pools financial resources from various public, private, and international institutions and acts as a credit agency offering long-term repayment schedules and low interest rates for new industrial concerns. The Industrial Development Corporation (CFI) is another government agency that acts as a financing agent assisting industries that seek to meet domestic consumer needs. The Dominican Institute of Industrial Technology (INDOTEC) has been established for (among other responsibilities) training workers in the skills necessary for an expanding industrial sector.

The desire to expand the industrial sector is further enhanced by the application of incentives established by Public Law 299. The essential elements of this law, passed in 1968, are shown below, providing a visual and graphic summary of how Dominican governments have sought to entice foreign capital and manufacturing to the country, employing substantial tax and import duty reductions as incentives.

The prospects for greater industrial growth in the Dominican Republic in the 1980s seem promising. With extensive support and financing from the government and continued interest from foreign investors, both because of the incentives and the low labor costs, manufacturing will likely continue to expand. But unlike Balaguer's, Guzmán's administration was convinced industrial growth should be accompanied

Table 8.1
Public Law 299: Incentives for Investment

DEFINITION OF CATEGORIES

For the purpose of granting the benefits and concessions provided by
Law No. 299, industrial activities have been classified in the three
categories designated A, B, and C.

A Industries engaged in the manufacture of products for the export
market only. Assembly plants fall into this category.

B All new industries of high priority to national development, especially those engaged in the manufacture of items not produced
in the country which are intended to replace imported products,
satisfying a demand of the domestic market.

C All new production or expansion of existing industries engaged
in the processing of local raw materials or in the manufacture
of products for domestic consumption.

INCENTIVES OFFERED	INDUSTRIAL CATEGORIES		
	A	B	C
Exemption from import duties and taxes on raw materials, semi-finished products or materials used in the composition or processing of the product, container or packing material.	100%	95%	Up to 90%
Exemption from import duties and taxes on machinery and equipment.	100%	---	---
Exemption from import duties and taxes on fuels and lubricants used strictly for industrial processing, except gasoline.	100%	95%	Up to 90%
Exemption from income tax.	100%	Up to 50% on investments	Up to 50% on investments

Class A, B and C industries enjoy the benefits of their classification
for the period of time indicated below in accordance with their geo-
graphical location. If the company is located:

in Santo Domingo	8 years
in Santiago	10 years
in a frontier zone	20 years
anywhere else in the country	15 years

20 year concessions are usually granted to Class A industries regardless of location.

by a parallel modernization of agriculture. In their view, industry and agriculture needed to be kept in balance.

THE PLACE OF SOCIAL WELFARE PROGRAMS IN A MODERNIZING ECONOMY

Even more serious than the dispute between agricultural and industrial policy priorities has been the debate over social welfare programs. At the core of the dispute is the reality of a poor country with limited resources and tight budgetary restrictions, as opposed to the rising public demand for greater spending on health care, housing, social security, and other essential human services.

The dilemma of allocating scarce government resources in a way that responds effectively to the social wants and needs of the population is one that will not be easily resolved. The Dominican government can put its limited capital into investments for the future or it can spend it on social programs that satisfy immediate needs, but it cannot do both. Hence, social welfare policy has become the most hotly contested issue in Dominican politics today. Starting with the 1978 presidential campaign, Dominican political leaders have been debating the proper balance of domestic priorities: investment versus consumption. Balaguer stood firm on his record as a builder and modernizer and pointed with pride at the budget figures for his years in office that showed a clear preference for spending for the armed forces and capital construction. But Balaguer also reminded Dominicans of the considerable budget increments of his administration for education.

Guzmán and the PRD, in contrast, promised less attention to construction and infrastructure development and more to social programs. But in office Guzmán found that such a reordering of spending priorities was not so easy. Key social and economic elites questioned the needs for expanded social programs and argued both that the country could not afford them and that longer-term economic development would have to be sacrificed.

An early dispute occurred over housing, a Guzmán priority. The president of the nation's Central Bank, a Balaguer supporter, blocked a government housing credit of $32 million on the grounds it was inflationary. The decision by the bank drew howls of protest from the PRD. Guzmán's own economic coordinator lashed out at the bank's decision as a failure to respond to legitimate social demands. Guzmán was caught in the middle. As the leader of the PRD, he sympathized with the frustration of fellow party members eager to carry out a key part of the party program. But as president, he recognized the necessity of maintaining balance, holding down inflation, and continuing to work amicably with powerful economic officials and institutions. In the end he fired his PRD advisor and bore the brunt of the party's criticism; the housing program was blocked.

The lesson of the housing controversy is that government actions to reorder national priorities in a situation of scarce resources cannot be separated from the realities of economic and political power. Whereas modernization in the industrial and agricultural sectors is something on which virtually all groups can agree (although obviously differing on priorities) and from which all can benefit, social welfare programs imply choices concerning which groups and classes will receive the major benefits from government programs. Social programs are designed primarily for the poor, who are the largest group numerically, but are politically (so far) the weakest in the country. They thus run up against the opposition of the economic elites who have other priorities and the political influence to back up their preferences.

It is against this backdrop of rising mass demands and expectations versus elite interests and power that the PRD and Guzmán had to formulate and implement policy in the social welfare area. Obviously, agricultural and industrial policy are important in terms of the country's long-range development, but social programs are also necessary both to relieve human suffering and to test a democratic government's capacity to achieve justice and a more equitable division of wealth and power. The balance is not easy to strike.

AUSTERITY AND THE QUALITY OF ECONOMIC GROWTH

Decisions on priorities and budget allocations in poor countries like the Dominican Republic are not easy. Most of them do not involve simple choices between moral good and evil, but choices between lesser evils. Likewise with the debate over austerity.

Austerity implies the putting off of benefits and consumption now for the sake of promised benefits in some distant and usually vague future. The burden of austerity falls generally on the shoulders of the poor. In the Dominican Republic, austerity measures have been used to restrict current consumption in order to generate greater capital for investment or other purposes. Balaguer used a variety of austerity measures during his tenure to control inflation and make available the necessary revenue for his development programs. For example, most strikes during Balaguer's rule were declared illegal, as a way of helping hold down wages. Food prices were allowed to rise as a means of cutting consumption. State workers were refused pay increases for the entire twelve years of Balaguer's rule. Only in 1979, under Guzmán, did the state workers finally get a pay raise along with a new law providing for a minimum wage of $125 a month, paid vacation time, and a guaranteed Christmas bonus.

Balaguer's austerity programs affected not just workers, but the aged, the poor, and the disabled as well. Pensions during Balaguer's presidency remained at $30 per month, even in the face of inflation at nearly 20 percent during some of those years. Programs for the disabled were also cut back. The Guzmán administration sought to improve conditions in the homes for the disabled and raised pensions to $100 a month, a great improvement over the previous figure but still paltry as a sum to try to live on.

Balaguer followed an intensive austerity program but Guzmán had to continue many of the same or similar policies. The decision by the government to raise gasoline prices from $1.25 to $1.85 per gallon in 1979 may have been necessary to reduce consumption and pay for foreign oil, but it was also a devastating blow to urban workers, jitney drivers, and truckers whose work requires cheap and available fuel. Guzmán's image as a man of the people was severely damaged as a result of the price hike decision and helped to reinforce the view of the left that Guzmán was a conservative oligarch in PRD clothing.

The use of austerity measures to curb inflation and finance modernization sparked new interest in the Dominican Republic's tax laws. Guzmán, seeking to assuage lower- and middle-class anger over regressive gasoline hikes, promised to reform the nation's tax system. Taxes in the Dominican Republic are woefully inequitable, collected sporadically, and heavily reliant on regressive import-export taxes rather than fairer property or income taxes. The beneficiaries of tax policy have been the middle and upper classes, who have received preferential treatment, while the poor continue to suffer and pay a disproportionate share of the tax bill.

The importance of the tax system as a public policy issue was also brought out in the 1978 election. When Balaguer saw that Guzmán was leading in the vote count, he sought to rally support for his position by firing the tax collector, whom many Dominicans thought of as "the most honest guy in the government." The ploy did not save Balaguer, but it did reveal his desire to retain middle- and upper-class support by using the sensitive taxation issue.

Officers directing traffic

Guzmán called tax reform a "top national priority" and made other statements suggesting that taxes might be collected more equitably and derived from a broader base, including higher property and income taxes. But rhetoric has so far outweighed actions. Significant steps toward tax reform would be a sign that the government views the costs of national development as a burden that must be borne equally and without preferential treatment. The changes in workers pay schedules and pensions already point to the government's awareness that the costs cannot and should not be shouldered by the poor indefinitely. But tax reform will be even more difficult because it strikes at the class system and hits people where it hurts most: property and pocketbook.

THREE POLICIES: POPULATION, ENERGY, EDUCATION

We have looked at agricultural policy, industrial policy, and welfare policy. It can be argued that success in these areas is dependent on success in other social policy areas, most notably family planning, energy policy, and educational policy. Indeed, posing the issue in this way serves to show how interrelated the vicious circles of Dominican underdevelopment are, and how intractable the problems are.

Population Policy

The Dominican Republic has long seen its population problems in terms of too small a population rather than too great a population. Emptied and depopulated during the colonial era, devastated still further during the Haitian occupation, and fearful subsequently that Haiti, with its greater numbers but less territory, would overwhelm the whole island, the policy of virtually all Dominican governments has been to seek to increase the population through immigration and incentives for large families.

Family planning did not emerge as a major issue until the 1960s. The first family planning efforts were carried out by private individuals, then the government made some weak and tentative efforts to encourage family planning, and finally, in 1968, the Balaguer government created a National Council on Population and the Family to oversee an official family planning program. Funds and planning for the program come almost exclusively from the United States.

The program remains controversial. The Church is opposed but has been persuaded to maintain a low profile. The left is opposed. So is the right, which wants to maintain a strong barrier against Haiti's possible intrusions and also wishes to keep a large, cheap labor supply. In addition, many poor Dominicans see large numbers of children as a means to increase family income by putting more hands in the field and as a form of social security insurance in old age.

But the government has been persuaded that its ambitious programs in housing, education, economic development and other areas will be in vain unless population growth is checked. Today it operates some 250 clinics, plus a considerable publicity campaign and some 2,000 community workers to go door-to-door, especially in poor and rural areas, to talk about health, nutrition, and family planning matters.

Since the 1960s, the population growth rate has fallen from about 3.5 percent per year to about 2.9 percent today. Some of this drop is due to the efforts of the government's family planning program, but at least equally important have been migration, chiefly to Puerto Rico and the United States, and such "natural" causes as education and urbanization, since in the cities large numbers of children make less sense than in the country. Hence, while the family planning program seems well established, the results in terms of actually reaching women of child-bearing age or of affecting significantly the population growth rate are still quite meager. Meanwhile the population pressures on the land, on social services, and on the whole social and political system have continued to build.

Energy Development

Much has been said about Dominican dependency and its effects on the country's internal economic situation. Although the dependency issue is often discussed in terms of trade and investment, perhaps the most critical area of Dominican dependence is its heavy reliance on foreign oil. Present energy imports exceed export revenues by $100 million yearly. The Dominicans are acutely conscious of this imbalance and are making adjustments, especially in tourism and manufacturing, as a way of increasing earnings to pay the ever-rising oil bill. Nevertheless, the domestic demand for oil has not abated, as population pressures and a more diversified economy create ever-greater need.

To meet the energy crisis, the Guzmán administration formed a special National Commission for Energy Policy, whose mission is to find "ways to reduce reliance on oil imports and to identify sectors where significant conservation can be achieved." To achieve this objective the government, through its energy agency, the Dominican Electric Power Corporation (CDE), began extensive oil exploration (conducted jointly with U.S. firms), research into the feasibility of using bagasse (the husks of sugar cane) as an energy source, and serious examination of solar energy, which many feel has a real future in that sun-drenched country.

Because this search for alternative energy sources is largely future-oriented, the government was also strongly involved in finding short-run answers to meet the country's more immediate needs. Early in 1980, Guzmán announced the commitment of $142 million for improvements in existing power systems and an agreement with Spain for planning studies on the proposed Higuey-El Aguacate dam, which would provide

The oil refinery at Haina

an additional 200 megawatts of power to meet the country's expanding needs.

The Dominican-Spanish agreement continues a pattern of energy development in the Dominican Republic that seeks to have the country's energy needs filled by tapping the scores of rivers that flow from the major mountain ranges. The development of hydroelectric power, Dominicans feel, enables them to harness energy from these rivers, and also aids the agricultural sector by channeling water to areas in need of irrigation. Such projects also help serve the water needs of the capital. The Madrigal Dam, when completed, will provide an additional 50,000 kw. of power to Santo Domingo and should also give its residents sufficient potable water until the year 2000.

The construction of hydroelectric dams has been one of the primary areas of international financial assistance to the Dominican Republic. Besides the long-standing interest of Spain in these projects, the government has also received assistance from the IADB, the World Bank, the United States Export-Import Bank, and other foreign commercial banks. Such outlays of foreign assistance have been used by the government to develop twenty-eight hydroelectric plants with more planned for the future.

The governmental efforts with respect to energy development are not as controversial as the family planning programs discussed above, but the problem is just as intractable and its resolution or successful management just as important for the continued modernization of the nation. Without a steady, reliable supply of energy, the prospects for increased industrialization and continued economic growth will be dim.

Educational Expansion

Although there have been many differences between the two recent Dominican administrations, Balaguer and Guzmán both shared a commitment to education. Both viewed education as an "engine" of progress and change. Guzmán, however, was even more committed to expanding educational opportunities than his predecessor. He called for the complete overhaul of the middle (roughly, junior high) school and for greater adult education programs in the country. The administration seemed most concerned about the continued high rate of illiteracy, a staggering drop-out rate after the first few years of school, and the paucity of vocational programs that are essential if the country is to meet the demands of increased industrialization.

The commitment of the Guzmán administration to education was not mere words. A comparison of the education appropriation for 1978 (Balaguer's last year) and 1979 (Guzmán's first year) points clearly to an expanded emphasis on education.

The Guzmán administration's budgetary increases for education produced quick results. In 1979, 490 new schools with a total of 1,000 classrooms were built at a cost of $16.7 million. Guzmán also began programs to increase opportunities for vocational education and to reduce illiteracy.

The pride that Guzmán took in such developments must be weighed against the increasing complexities of providing educational reform in a modernizing society. Building schools is only part of the solution; the more serious difficulties involve staffing and equipping the schools, keeping children in the classroom, and training them for a job market that is highly uncertain. These problems of retaining students and creating jobs for them are of course related to the even larger uncertainties concerning the future of the economy. So far, the government has been quite successful in the comparatively easy tasks of securing funds and putting up buildings; but the harder tasks of teaching useful and relevant skills, reducing illiteracy, founding trade schools, and

Table 8.2
Educational Appropriations: Balaguer and Guzmán Compared

	1978 (Balaguer)	1979 (Guzmán)
Total Education millions of $	72.3	116.4
Elementary and Secondary	41.8	67.7
Higher Education	2.1	4.3
Total Budget	620.4	736.7
% for education in total budget	11.65%	15.80%

matching educational programs with the economic and developmental needs of the country – rather than simply producing more waifs to shine shoes or sell fruit – are yet to be accomplished.

PUBLIC POLICY AND THE FUTURE OF DOMINICAN DEVELOPMENT

The Dominican Republic has modernized a great deal in the last two decades, and the significant progress achieved in various public policy fields bodes well for the future. Yet one must not think of this development as inevitable or unilinear. Setbacks and reversals are always possible, the external environment may upset even the best-conceived plans, and the play of internal political and social forces may yet produce chaos and breakdown.

The Dominican Republic, first and foremost, is a poor, underdeveloped, and dependent nation. It is dependent economically in the sense that it must rely on external markets to sell and buy its goods, and it is dependent politically and militarily as a small nation lying within what the United States considers its sphere of influence. This external dependency affects the country's ability to sustain its developmental efforts. With revenue, investment capital, trade and technology all dependent on decisions and forces made or located outside its borders, the government must devote at least as much attention to these external pressures as to the internal ones. It is subject to a host of pressures and changes that it has no capacity to control.

As modern Dominican history attests, when the external context is favorable, considerable internal development can also occur. But when such "dependency variables" as declining sugar revenues, increased prices for oil, inflated prices for imported manufactured goods, reduced capital investment, shortages of technical equipment also imported from the outside, or U.S. disfavor of a regime or policy are introduced into the picture, the country may not only experience delays and sometimes severe setbacks in its development efforts, but its fragile political system may be destabilized as well.

The often damaging impact of these "dependency variables," coupled with uncertain "governing variables," can make Dominican development extremely shaky and uncertain. Deep-seated political divisions, a sometimes interventionist military, ineffective or corrupt administration, and a weak system of representative government have created a public policy environment that is extremely tenuous. The effective implementation of worthwhile public policies cannot be very successfully carried out in a climate of suspicion, distrust, fear, antagonism, and divisionism.

The solution, of course, would be a happy mix of "dependency" and "governing" variables, but Dominican public policy in the contemporary era has not generally operated in such a favorable climate. Under Balaguer the Dominican Republic was led by a man for whom the dependency variables, i.e., relations with the outside world, high sugar prices, etc., were unusually favorable. Balaguer was able to achieve his economic "miracle" precisely because these external conditions were so propitious, and because the surpluses generated could be used to keep the "governing variables" in check, i.e., the economic pie was sufficiently large and expanding that many who might otherwise go into opposition could also share in the pieces.

Balaguer's "miracle" eventually turned into a disaster as a result of the reversal of precisely the same factors that had created the original boom. By 1974, sugar prices had plummeted, oil prices skyrocketed, and investment income slackened off. Growth rates that had been in the 9-12 percent range dropped to 4-5 percent. These external economic and "dependency" forces caused a massive downturn in the economy and, with a smaller pie to cut up, also activated the "governing variables," the internal political opposition forces that accelerated the decline of the Balaguer regime. Balaguer, the once secure builder and modernizer of Dominican society who had enjoyed widespread support, now faced angry crowds, a restive military, charges of malfeasance, and a renewed political challenge from a worthy opponent.

Guzmán wrestled with these same dependency and governing forces, and had to weigh carefully the impact they would have on the prospects for both economic development and political stability. The external "dependency" variables largely control the overall pace and quality of Dominican modernization, and these in turn help shape the internal, more immediate, "governing" variables and forces, which are capable of overthrowing a government.

It must always be remembered that in the Dominican Republic the probability of rapid change is extremely high in both the external and the internal conditions, which makes the tenure of any government very uncertain. A clever and prudent president can manage some of these forces through his own initiatives, but if he is realistic he will also recognize that some of them are entirely out of his hands. That is also true of the Dominican public policy process in general: it is in large part subject to forces, external and internal, that are only partially predictable and controllable, and that may offer very few clues as to the extent of their impact on either economic or political development.

9

The Dominican Republic in the International Arena

One of the most fascinating aspects of the Dominican Republic is the high level of visibility – whether through its own efforts or as a victim of the actions of other nations – that it has maintained in the international arena throughout its history. Other countries in Latin America with larger populations or land areas have not been at the center stage of world politics as often as the Dominican Republic has. Unfortunately, the worldwide visibility, or perhaps notoriety, of the Dominican Republic has in many instances not been the result of its own initiatives, but the result of foreign intervention in its internal affairs, its dependency relations, or its tumultuous internal politics. The Dominican Republic has an international importance all out of proportion to its size, population, or resources.

Because of its location the nation has historically been of major strategic significance. Hispaniola is the second largest island in the Caribbean. It lies athwart the major trade routes from Europe to the Caribbean and Central America, and from the U.S. east coast to the Panama Canal and all of South America. From the sixteenth through the eighteenth centuries, when the Caribbean was one of the world's most important imperial frontiers, all the major powers – Spain, France, England, Holland – sought to conquer Hispaniola. The United States is only the most recent in a long history of great powers that have tried to dominate the island and the Dominican Republic.

DOMINICAN–UNITED STATES RELATIONS

The importance of the Dominican Republic to the United States stems in large part from its strategic geographic position in the Caribbean and the long-standing view of the United States that the Caribbean is in *its* sphere of influence and must be protected. The attitude that the

125

Caribbean is an "American back yard" and its southern first line of defense has been held by all American presidents since James Monroe. Uncomfortable in the face, successively, of a French, British, Spanish, German, and most recently Soviet presence so close to its shores, the United States has repeatedly intervened in the internal affairs of its weak Caribbean neighbors. With few reservations and no respect for the sovereignty of the Dominican Republic, U.S. presidents have threatened and cajoled, "negotiated" trade and lending arrangements manifestly unfair to the Dominican Republic, administered and collected for itself that nation's export revenues, advocated full annexation as a means of guaranteeing domination, and on two eventful occasions sent the U.S. Marines to occupy the country and redirect the course of its history.

The Dominican Republic in many respects has become a major symbol of Latin American vulnerability to foreign, in particular U.S., domination. Latin Americans see in the Dominican Republic the sad results of proximity to the "colossus of the north." Even though many Latin American countries have experienced foreign intervention or dependent economic relations, or have become pawns in world conflict, the Dominican Republic stands most prominently as a nation whose historical unfolding has been a constant reminder of the power of outside forces.

The relationship of the United States to the Dominican Republic can best be described as one of "suprasovereignty." The term "suprasovereignty" is used here because it conveys the idea that the United States not only reacts to internal Dominican events in ways that alter its politics and development, but also makes decisions affecting the Dominican Republic as if it (the United States) were sovereign. From the days of Grant's attempted annexation to Roosevelt's customs receivorship, to Wilson's occupations, Kennedy's interventions, Johnson's sending of the Marines, and Carter's human rights policy, the United States has viewed the Dominican Republic not as an independent nation but as a dependency or satellite. The United States has repeatedly sought to place its stamp on the course of Dominican history.

From the perspective of the United States, its "suprasovereignty" in the Dominican Republic has had a positive impact on Dominican society. As numerous American presidents and policymakers have sought to emphasize, U.S. action also brought, at times, stability, economic growth, and modernization to the Dominicans. Many Dominicans also recognize the advantages of these ties, which help explain their love-hate attitudes toward the United States. But many are also concluding that in this unequal relationship the United States has been the major beneficiary, using the Dominican Republic as a pawn in the international power struggle and as a source of needed resources. The Dominicans view the United States as the ultimate arbiter of their destiny and as the prime beneficiary of an unequal "partnership."

In the contemporary period the foreign policy issues of U.S.-Dominican relations have revolved around anticommunism and, to a lesser extent, the desire to create a model of liberalism and democracy in the Caribbean. With the rise of the cold war and the fear of Soviet expansionism, the United States sought allies in Latin America who would champion the cause of anticommunism. In dictator Rafael Trujillo, the United States found a staunch "anticommunist" and rewarded him for his loyalty and vigilance with lucrative trade and aid packages and tacit acceptance of his dictatorial regime. In turn, Trujillo posed as "the best friend of the United States in Latin America" and the "foremost anticommunist in the hemisphere." But when Trujillo overreached himself and it looked like his regime was coming to an end, the United States turned against its long-time ally and sought to pursue its anticommunism in another form.

The United States under John F. Kennedy sought to preserve stability and prevent communism not by aid to dictators but by supporting liberal democrats. It was reasoned that a liberal-democratic reform program was a better defense against communism than a right wing dictator (the example of Batista in Cuba was in everyone's mind) who would create or perpetuate the conditions under which communism might thrive. In Juan Bosch the United States thought it had found a democratic alternative to Castroism. Unfortunately for Bosch and liberal democracy, U.S. support was half-hearted and easily overcome. When Bosch angered conservatives by appearing "soft" on leftists, the United States turned away and allowed its "experiment in democracy" to give way to a military coup.

The anticommunism of the United States was dominated by the "no second Cuba" doctrine. U.S. officials were adamant that "Castro-communism" not be allowed to spread further in Latin America. Hence when the Dominicans launched their revolution in 1965 to restore constitutional democracy, but which U.S. officials thought might produce a Castro-like regime, the United States intervened militarily to prevent the revolution from succeeding.

The defeat of the constitutionalist movement and the manipulation that helped produce Joaquín Balaguer's electoral victory showed the world, and particularly the Dominicans, the depth of the United States' fear of communism (or what was thought to be communism) and how far the United States would go to prevent it. To many in the United States, the intervention achieved a double "success": a potentially pro-Castro government was prevented from coming to power with minimal losses of American lives and in a relatively short period of time (in contrast to the Viet Nam imbroglio), while the new leadership these events produced (Balaguer) was pro-American and presented an image of moderate democracy. Most Dominicans, of course, saw the intervention in quite another light.

During Balaguer's return to "normalcy," 1966–1978, the anticommunist issue remained largely dormant. There was considerable U.S. assistance in the early years to help the Dominican Republic recover from the devastation of the revolution, but after that the Dominican Republic was essentially ignored. Relations between the two countries were dominated mainly by economic issues (trade, aid, sugar prices), not by the "hotter" political controversies of the immediate past. Through its assistance the United States helped prop up the Balaguer government, and Balaguer was clever at manipulating the United States to gain advantages for himself.

The 1978 election campaign between Balaguer and Guzmán revived the issues of both Castro's Cuba and whether liberal democracy or authoritarianism was the best defense against communism in the Dominican Republic. The foreign policy issue of major concern in the campaign was whether Cuba should be recognized. Some of Guzmán's initial speeches suggested that the country should rethink its earlier break in diplomatic and economic relations with Cuba. But while Guzmán seemed interested in merely exploring the issue, leftists in the PRD, like Peña Gómez, were promoting recognition of Cuba as a major plank in the party's platform.

The Cuba issue was eventually overshadowed by the military's efforts to halt the ballot count and suppress the issue of whether democracy in the Dominican Republic would even survive. With the outcome hanging in the balance, President Carter acted to support Guzmán and his claim of victory. Threatening to cut off aid, and strongly supporting the principle of democratic choice, Carter was able to intimidate Balaguer and the military and to guarantee a democratic outcome.

The position taken by Carter seemed a refreshing departure from the past, but one must be careful not to overstate the differences. Dominicans and Latin Americans alike joined in praise of the U.S. action. But in retrospect, it should be noted that the vigorous defense of democracy by Carter was made easier by the absence of any perceived communist threat at the time. It has always been easy for the United States to support democracy during such noncrisis times; it is in revolutionary and unstable circumstances when the actors are not so well

known and the outcomes more uncertain, that the United States is prone
to support the other side. And it is likely that, given Balaguer's advanced
age and infirmity, the United States perceived Guzmán as a safer defense
against communism than the possible chaos after Balaguer's demise.

Furthermore, even in this case the role played by the United States
was in keeping with the relationship of "suprasovereignty." The United
States had again taken decisive steps to influence the course of
Dominican history. Without Carter's actions, it is likely that Guzmán
would not have been inaugurated as president. But whatever its political
preferences in that specific matter, the United States had again
demonstrated its omnipotence in shaping Dominican outcomes.

To a large extent, therefore, the future of U.S.-Dominican relations
depends on issues and circumstances beyond the Dominicans' control.
But it also depends on the actions of Dominican leaders. Guzmán
pleased U.S. officials when he refused to recognize Cuba or to nationalize Gulf and Western. But within Dominican governing circles
there are pressures to move in these directions, and also many signs of
disenchantment with the United States over trade and aid policies. The
Dominican government is very critical of the United States for refusing
to reduce trade barriers for Dominican exports and for its insufficient
aid, especially in response to the damage caused by Hurricane David.

In the final analysis, Dominican-U.S. relations will depend on
larger issues than aid or trade. The bedrocks of U.S. policy remain the
same: internal stability, anticommunism, and regional security. As long
as the Dominican government follows this line, U.S. interests in the
country will be largely peripheral and concerned with technical and
generally noncontroversial matters, as in the Balaguer years. But if the
seeds of social revolution again blossom or the specter of Castro-
communism looms, it is unlikely that the United States will stand by
quietly.

DOMINICAN RELATIONS WITH ITS CLOSEST NEIGHBORS

Haiti and Puerto Rico

Although the United States remains the center of most Dominican
international attention, there are longer and potentially as important
relationships that the Dominican Republic maintains with its most prox-
imate neighbors, Haiti to the west and Puerto Rico to the east.

Dominican-Haitian relations have seldom been cordial. The
Dominican Republic has been invaded, occupied, and pillaged by the
Haitians on numerous occasions since the beginning of the nineteenth

century. Haiti in turn accuses the Dominican Republic of being a racist nation, slaughtering unwanted Haitians (20,000–30,000 during the Trujillo era), and continuing to import and use Haitians as almost slave laborers. These attitudes have been hardened by stereotypes and have produced hostility, antagonism, and warlike competition.

Although much of the animosity stems from this history of conflict, occupations, and racial prejudice, the more recent problems between the two nations have their roots in a different set of conditions: Dominican development in the face of Haitian stagnation. In the last several decades the Dominican Republic has made great strides, while Haiti has remained the most underdeveloped nation in Latin America. The autocratic Duvalier family, which has been in power in Haiti since the 1950s, has been unable or unwilling to raise the country's living standards and has used exceedingly repressive tactics to stay in power.

The regime of Jean Claude "Bebe Doc" Duvalier did little to solve that nation's immense problems. Overpopulated, denuded of trees and topsoil, its agriculture largely ruined, Haiti is a quasi-"basket case." Its depressed conditions put immense pressures on the Dominican Republic next door. Though the border between the two countries is officially closed, thousands of Haitians continue to stream across. Many are brought in to cut cane. Though legally obliged to return to Haiti, few do so because job opportunities and salaries are so much better on the Dominican side. As illegal immigrants, they have been assimilated into the Dominican population.

Recently the issue of slave labor has been raised. A U.N. study alleges that nearly 12,000 Haitian cane cutters per year are sold to the Dominicans at eleven dollars a head. The report goes on to describe the conditions of "extreme squalor and depravity" under which the Haitians live in several Dominican labor camps. The study claims the traffic in cane cutters is condoned by both the Haitian and Dominican governments, to the extent of their working out an agreement on the fee paid for each Haitian worker rounded up and sent to the Dominican Republic.

Despite the tensions created by illegal immigration and the charges of collusion in what is almost a slave trade, the two governments have sought to develop better relations. For the first time since 1958, the two countries' leaders met in 1979 to discuss their common problems and common interests. Presidents Duvalier and Guzmán signed an agreement of cooperation and discussed the use of Dominican territory as a base for anti-Duvalier guerrilla attacks. Subsequently they met again to open a new irrigation project benefiting both countries.

The talks and agreements do not mean the antagonisms between the two countries that have existed for some two centuries have been resolved. The differences between the two governments, especially in the areas of trade and human rights, are great; the differences between the two nations and peoples, in language, culture, racial attitudes and composition, are even greater. But it is important to recognize a significant shift in Dominican foreign policy toward Haiti. Guzmán sought to expand commerce with his neighbor and to lessen the racial and cultural antagonisms that lie at the root of their strained relations. The two governments have recently created a fund of $1 million to be used to increase trade. The racial-cultural differences between them may be lessened over time, but attitudes that have been held so long will not quickly or easily disappear.

Future relations between the two countries are tied closely to the future of the Duvalier regime. If internal instability besets Haiti, the Dominican Republic is almost certain to be drawn into the conflict. Such involvement is sure to rekindle the old animosities between two neighbors who have on a number of occasions been close to war. At the same time, Haiti's continued nondevelopment, the differences in living standards between the two countries, and illegal immigration into the Dominican Republic also help preserve the age-old prejudices.

Although Dominicans still feel little identification with Haiti, they do have much in common with the neighboring Puerto Ricans. The Dominican Republic has had a long and generally amicable relationship with Puerto Rico. The two islands are separated by a short hop by plane or boat. The Dominicans and Puerto Ricans speak the same language, share the same culture, and vacation or shop on each other's island.

But trade is also a major factor in their relations. Puerto Rico consistently ranks high in import and export trade with the Dominican Republic. Figures for 1976–1977 show Puerto Rico fourth as a buyer of Dominican exports, behind only the United States, Switzerland, and the Netherlands. Puerto Rico also is a major supplier of Dominican imports.

The cordial relations between the Dominicans and the Puerto Ricans should not imply that there are no areas of disagreement or concern. Over the years, fishing limits have provided one bone of contention. The rich Cabo Engaño and Siete Hermanos fishing beds off the coast of the Dominican Republic are worked by both Puerto Rican and Dominican fishermen. The competition has been sufficiently fierce that the U.S. government entered the controversy to work out an acceptable compromise. Dominican leaders tend to play down the disagreement, but the issues of fishing rights and catch ceilings, especially since the prime fishing areas are within the two hundred mile limits of both islands, require constant monitoring by the government.

An issue with even more explosive potential is the disparity in living standards between the two islands and, hence, the large number of Dominicans who have migrated to Puerto Rico. San Juan, Puerto Rico, is now thought to be the fourth largest "Dominican" city, behind only Santo Domingo, Santiago, and New York. An estimated 100,000 Dominicans (probably considerably more, since many have entered illegally, coming across the Mona Passage by boat at night) have settled in the Commonwealth of Puerto Rico, from which a considerable proportion emigrate again, this time to New York. This last step in the migration process is probably the easiest; to go from Puerto Rico to New York requires only money, credit, or a paid passage – not visas or immigration papers.

Former President Bosch, who himself spent four years of political exile in Puerto Rico, bemoans the deterioration of life in his country that makes such a massive exodus of Dominicans to Puerto Rico or the United States an economic necessity. Although Bosch's comments are connected with his hope that these economic exiles might constitute a force for triggering revolutionary change back in the Dominican Republic, it is important to remember that the Dominicans in Puerto Rico also pose problems for the Commonwealth. Despite the much higher per-capita income figures in Puerto Rico ($2,250 per year, as compared with the Dominican Republic's $850), the Commonwealth also is faced with high unemployment, overextended welfare costs, and acute shortages of housing and human services. The Dominicans living in Puerto Rico thus compete for scarce jobs and services with a population that can ill afford new arrivals. Frequently the Dominicans take jobs away from Puerto Ricans because they are willing to work for less. This competition and potential for ugly conflict concern both Dominicans and Puerto Ricans.

The issue of Puerto Rico's status is also of major interest to the Dominicans. Most government officials, including the president, have not taken a formal stand on the three options open to Puerto Rico – commonwealth, statehood, or independence – preferring to state publicly that it is up to the Puerto Ricans to decide for themselves. Most conservative and centrist Dominicans, however, favor either statehood or a continuation of the commonwealth status, which would have the practical effect of maintaining or increasing the United States presence and commitment in the Caribbean. In contrast, the left wing of the PRD, and leftists in general, support independence for Puerto Rico and are critical of the continuing colonial arrangement that the United States maintains with Puerto Rico. This element clearly favors a diminution of U.S.

presence in the Caribbean—though neither group appears to have thought through the full economic and pragmatic implications of its position.

SOCIALISM AND DOMINICAN FOREIGN POLICY: WHAT DIRECTIONS?

Although Dominican foreign policy has traditionally been oriented toward enhancing or adjusting its relations with its immediate neighbors—Haiti, the United States, Puerto Rico, sometimes Venezuela or Cuba—in recent years broader issues and a grander ideological vision have also taken hold. For the first time since Bosch and the revolution of 1965, attention has been focused by the PRD-Guzmán administration on the larger global issues of international politics. The debate concerns the changing relations of power and influence in the world and, more specifically, the precise model of socialism that the Dominican Republic should emulate and the attendant shifts in trade and diplomatic relations that would likely accompany such a shift.

The issue of "which form of socialism" has moved to center stage because of the distinct positions taken within the dominant PRD. President Guzmán, along with such leaders as Salvador Jorge Blanco and Jacobo Majluta, represented the more moderate wing of the party that has consistently viewed itself as socialist in the mold of the European social-democrats. This group believes in parliamentary democracy, a mixed economy combining private and public ownership, and a foreign policy aligned with, let us say, the left wing of the U.S. Democratic Party.

The leftists in the PRD, particularly younger ex-student and labor leaders, who are led by its Secretary-General Peña Gómez and Chamber of Deputies President Hatuey de Camps, define socialism more in terms of the Yugoslav, Cuban, and now Nicaraguan models. Neither Peña nor de Camps are Leninists, but they are ideological Marxists, and both feel strongly that the Dominican Republic should follow the lead of these more radical socialist regimes in nationalizing concerns like Gulf and Western, pursuing more revolutionary domestic policies, reestablishing relations with Cuba, opening up greater contact with the socialist countries, and breaking out of some of its dependency relations with the United States.

The differences within the PRD over the correct interpretation of socialism have led to some bitter and divisive confrontations. After Guzmán took office, one of his first acts was to deal with Peña Gómez, who, in speaking to foreign journalists, had led them to believe the new government would soon explore an opening to Cuba. Peña's remarks were immediately repudiated by Guzmán, who made it clear he would be making foreign policy and the PRD secretary-general would not.

Despite continued pressure from the PRD left wing, Guzmán followed a moderate course. Instead of restoring formal diplomatic relations with Cuba, the Dominican Republic has permitted a number of unofficial ties. Sporting contests, cultural exchanges, and professional conferences involving Cubans and Dominicans have been encouraged. The government pointed with satisfaction to this developing relationship and concluded it was the best course to follow at the time. Guzmán, however, was conscious of the U.S. position on Cuba and the support he received from President Carter in 1978. The pressure on Guzmán from the left within his own party was outweighed by the support he required from the United States to advance his modernization plans and, perhaps, even to ward off potential military coups.

The decision by Guzmán to refrain from formal recognition of Cuba did not silence those favoring stronger ties. Hurricane David offered them further opportunity. Although most of the Hurricane assistance to rebuild the devastated country came from the United States, Venezuela, Colombia, and the OAS, a shipment of Cuban aid was also arranged by Peña, de Camps, and PRD President Jorge Blanco, without Guzmán's authorization. When the plane with the relief materials arrived in Santo Domingo along with the Cuban ministers of public health and higher education, Guzmán refused to meet the delegation and criticized the PRD leaders who had arranged the aid without his approval.

While PRD leftists tried to nudge the government toward a more radical form of socialism, Guzmán sought to align it closely with European social-democracy. He extolled the advantages of democratic reform socialism, and contrasted this with the economic failures of Cuba. Good relations were cultivated with the German Social Democratic Party and the Scandinavian socialists, and the PRD has been an active member of the Socialist International. There is a steady influx of European socialists into Santo Domingo for conferences, and PRD members regularly attend European meetings, where the Dominican Republic is viewed as one of the last remaining bastions of democratic socialism in Latin America.

The debate within the PRD between its left and right wings is certain to continue. For every speech delivered by Peña Gómez praising Cuba's accomplishments, Guzmán countered with an invitation to German Chancellor Helmut Schmidt or former Chancellor Willy Brandt to visit Santo Domingo. For every maneuver by Peña, who is the Socialist International representative for Latin America, to attract attention to programs of radical social change, Guzmán responded with praise of democratic and constitutional government. In this way, the ideological identity of the Guzmán government and the PRD was being shaped not so much by domestic issues or pressures, but in response to the question of which foreign model of socialism will prove dominant within the leadership and in shaping their plans for national development. If this controversy is resolved at some point it will have profound implications for the Dominican Republic and for its foreign policy and relations with the United States.

THE DOMINICAN REPUBLIC IN RELATION
TO THE CARIBBEAN AND THE WORLD

Dominican foreign policy is primarily regional and has historically involved relations mainly with the United States and the Spanish-speaking nations in and around the Caribbean. However, in recent years there has been a surge of new nations in the Caribbean, primarily former British colonies but some former French and Dutch territories as well. This has plunged the Dominican Republic into the larger maelstrom of Caribbean politics. Concurrently, its role in the hemisphere and world at large has also expanded.

Since the 1960s, the Dominican Republic has greatly expanded its international and diplomatic relations. It now has diplomatic relations with over fifty nations, in Latin America (all the countries except Cuba), Western Europe (all the major countries and most of the smaller ones), the Middle East (Israel and Lebanon), and Asia (Japan, Taiwan, South Korea). There are currently no formal diplomatic relations with any of the communist countries, though there are pressures in this direction and some limited commercial ties are being established.

The Dominican Republic has moved recently to increase its trade with such Latin American nations as Brazil, Mexico, and Venezuela. Of particular interest was the petroleum importation agreement signed with Venezuela, under which the Dominican Republic was given guarantees of uninterrupted supply and favorable loan arrangements to purchase oil. In its expanded ties with Mexico and Brazil, the Dominican Republic is also seeking to diversify its trade and reduce its dependence on Middle Eastern oil. But the Dominicans are proceeding cautiously in expanding trade with Latin America: They have refused to join the Latin American Free Trade Association (LAFTA), preferring to work out trade arrangements on a bilateral basis rather than through the larger multilateral agency.

The Dominican Republic has also expanded its diplomatic and

trade relations with a number of the small island nations that previously were crown colonies of Britain. The Dominicans recognize the rising importance of these small states in the area of trade and from the standpoint of political and strategic concerns. A revolutionary government in Grenada, Jamaica's deep political and ideological divisions, and the ferment caused by black power, national liberation, and decolonization movements throughout the small islands have forced the Dominicans to turn greater attention to these areas. However, as in the case of LAFTA, the Dominican Republic has not joined CARICOM, the Caribbean Common Market, preferring to deal bilaterally with nations such as Barbados, Trinidad-Tobago, and Jamaica.

Even with these new Caribbean and Latin American ties, the Dominican Republic has also intensified its efforts to expand its trade with Japan and Western Europe. The prosperity of these nations has given the Dominican Republic the opportunity to diversify its trade and to reduce somewhat its dependence on the United States. Expanded trade has been primarily with Canada, Japan, West Germany, The Netherlands, Switzerland, Italy, and Spain; these nations have also considerably expanded their investments, primarily in industry, construction, and mineral exploration, in the Dominican Republic.

The Dominican Republic has supplemented its bilateral relations with substantial involvement in international organizations. The Dominican Republic is a member of the U.N., the OAS, the U.N. Economic Commission for Latin America, the International Labor Organization (ILO), the International Court of Justice, and the IADB. It is also a participant in such financial and business agencies as the International Monetary Fund, the World Bank, the International Finance Corporation, the International Bauxite Association, and the Latin American and Caribbean sugar exporters' group. The last two are international cartels of commodity-producing nations which hope to do for bauxite and sugar what OPEC has done for oil.

It is instructive in seeking to understand the Dominican Republic's place in the international sphere to examine the important role it has played in one of these international agencies. The OAS, founded in 1948 as a regional arm of the U.N., is charged with helping maintain peace in the hemisphere and promoting economic and social development. The Dominican Republic is a charter member. What is most interesting about the OAS in the present study is the extraordinary amount of attention it has devoted to the Dominican Republic.

No other country except Cuba has been the focus of so much OAS, and thus hemispheric, attention as the Dominican Republic. In 1960, because of dictator Trujillo's efforts to assassinate the president of

Venezuela, the OAS for the first time imposed economic and diplomatic sanctions on a member nation. In 1962, after lifting the sanctions, the OAS provided assistance in rewriting Dominican electoral laws and in overseeing the election. In 1963 the OAS interposed itself between the Dominican Republic and Haiti when the two nations seemed on the brink of war. In 1965 the OAS, in what some have called its "darkest hour," submitted to intense U.S. pressure in agreeing to create the Inter-American Peace Force, which helped control the Dominican Revolution and provided a facade of hemispheric multilateralism to what was really a unilateral U.S. intervention. In 1978 the OAS was again involved in Dominican affairs when it protested the seizure of the ballot boxes by Balaguer supporters.

The OAS gained much of its experience in international peace-keeping, the application of sanctions, etc., through its various Dominican experiences. Many Dominicans would have preferred that such experience be acquired at the expense of another country.

RECENT TRENDS IN DOMINICAN FOREIGN POLICY

The Dominican Republic has been the center of much international controversy in the past, but in recent years it has sought to project the image of a peace maker and regional leader. During the most intense fighting of the Nicaraguan revolution in 1978–1979, for instance, the Dominican government participated in the ill-fated attempt to bring dictator Somoza and the Sandinista rebels together as a means of halting the destruction and bloodshed. This role was hotly criticized in the Dominican Republic because of the United States' role in sponsoring this action and suspicions that any agreement would enable Somoza to remain in power.

In response, Dominican officials viewed the Nicaraguan crisis as an opportunity to influence that revolution in a peaceful manner that would avoid intervention, so unlike the unhappy experience in their own country in 1965. But when the U.S.-sponsored talks broke down and the Sandinistas defeated Somoza, the Dominican government showed its sympathies by becoming one of the first countries to recognize the new government. Seeking to separate itself from the United States, the Guzmán government praised the revolution and welcomed the Sandinista leaders to Dominican soil.

The increased participation of the Dominican Republic in the Latin American community of nations, its democratic government, and the success of the Guzmán administration lifted the country to a position of prominence it had not enjoyed since the days of Juan Bosch. In a 1979 survey, conducted by a New York research firm, of 208 government, academic, and business leaders in the United States, the Dominican Republic was rated the second most important country in the Caribbean, behind only Cuba. President Guzmán was, that year, listed as the fourth most important political figure in the region, behind Castro, Jamaica's Manley (defeated in the recent elections), and President José López Portillo of Mexico. But Guzmán was only a scant 1 percent behind López Portillo, and significantly ahead of Venezuela's Luís Herrera Campins.

Such recognition is enormously important to the Dominicans, who take great pride in their nation having finally achieved its place in the sun. National recognition, in turn, reflects the stability, economic development, and democratic government achieved in the late 1970s, of which the Dominicans are also immensely proud.

The increased prominence and involvement of the Dominican Republic in Latin American affairs comes at an interesting time. As a result of the many island mini-states now receiving independence, the Nicaraguan revolution, the impending controversy over Puerto Rico's status, the economic difficulties of Cuba and Jamaica, and revolutionary upheaval in Guatemala and El Salvador, the Caribbean has surged to the forefront of attention in the United States and in world affairs.

As our title implies, the Dominican Republic lies in the center of this Caribbean crucible. Once again the Caribbean is viewed as having immense strategic importance, not only because of its proximity to the United States, its growing turmoil, and Cuba's efforts once more to export its revolution, but also because of the region's vast resources. In the near future the Caribbean islands and the mainland countries bordering it will become even more important than they already are as principal centers for the mining of gold, silver, and bauxite and for the extraction of that resource essential to everyone's well-being, oil.

Despite the attention it has received recently, the Caribbean has not exploded yet. But should the area become a major world "hot spot," the Dominican Republic will become of even greater strategic and political importance than it is at present. It is already being pressured to assume a leadership position as a means of providing needed direction and ameliorating harmful conflict. This does not mean the Dominican Republic will suddenly become a major regional power, but it does help emphasize what is already a reality: the recognition of the country as a significant regional influence, a model of democratic development, a force for stability in a region in turmoil.

With the growing importance of the Caribbean and the potential for major upheaval there, the Dominican Republic must be careful to avoid again becoming a pawn in the cold war between the communist nations and the United States. Already there are those in Washington who wish to use the Dominican Republic as a U.S.-favored "alternative" to communist Cuba or revolutionary Nicaragua. Additionally, the movement of more of the small islands in a Marxist direction would elevate the Dominican Republic to an even greater position of importance along what has been dubbed the "coconut curtain." As a democratic state, the Dominican Republic would be under great pressure to help counter this trend. But having seen its independence compromised so often in the past, and frequently caught up before in cold war issues that were peripheral to its interests and resulted in immense damage being done to the nation, many Dominicans would like to avoid being caught up in such controversies. A fresh conflict between the United States and the Soviet Union or Cuba, with such ingredients as Mexican and Venezuelan oil, Puerto Rican independence, Jamaican bauxite, and Central American revolution thrown in to complicate matters, could well destroy the stability, democracy, and modernization the Dominicans have achieved.

The international position of the Dominican Republic provides both problems and opportunities. The initiatives of the Guzmán government laid the groundwork for amicable relations with neighboring countries and strengthened the nation's own position in the region and the world. But the emergence of the Caribbean as an area of renewed importance and potential danger puts the Dominican Republic in a precarious spot. It may mean a chance for the country to further its stature and influence, or it may force it into an ideological and superpower struggle that could threaten its independence and recent accomplishments, and force it to reevaluate its crucial relationship with the United States.

10

Conclusion

The Dominican Republic has had a troubled past. Its considerable natural resources were milked dry by the Spaniards, and its native Indian population was decimated. It then suffered through some three centuries of colonial neglect, during which its institutions and political forms decayed and its social and economic structures reverted to more primitive subsistence forms. Manipulated and bartered by the great powers, both historically and presently, it has seldom had control of its own destiny.

Its history as an independent nation is as tumultuous and ruinous as its colonial history. First it was occupied and devastated by the Haitians. Then a succession of domestic tyrants—Santana, Báez, Heureaux, Trujillo—dominated its politics and its national life, with often disastrous consequences for the country. In between, there were occupations by Spain and the United States, immense internal turmoil, an occasional ineffective democratic leader, and a lack of economic development.

After Trujillo's assassination, the Dominicans again sought to achieve democratic growth. But the government was overthrown after only seven months, graft and oppression reappeared, and in 1965 the country exploded in revolution and civil war—only to see its hopes for a democratic restoration crushed once more by U.S. intervention.

The Dominican Republic remains a poor country. The gaps between rich and poor are vast. It has immense social and economic problems. Its resources are terribly limited. It is vulnerable to forces over which it has no control.

But the Dominicans are a proud and persevering people. In the past twenty years they have made immense strides. On a slim resource base, still heavily dependent on the United States, they have nevertheless made enormous progress toward economic development, social reform, and political democracy. This progress, in the face of the severe problems they must overcome or live with, has been both remarkable and heroic.

The accomplishments of the past two decades are still tenuous, however, and the situation could change very rapidly. The threats to democracy, from the armed forces and reactionary elements, are strong and very real. The country remains torn by social tensions and divisions. The economy remains precarious and would suffer devastating blows if oil prices increased dramatically or if sugar prices declined. Despite all its efforts at development and diversification, the economy is still subject to the whims of world market prices.

While the Dominican Republic has changed a great deal in the last twenty years, the question of whether these changes have been sufficient to alter its basic behavioral patterns must remain an open one. For instance, the two historical currents that have always vied for dominance in Dominican politics, the authoritarian one and the liberal-democratic one, are both still very much alive (as personified by the governments of Trujillo and Bosch, or Balaguer and Guzmán); one could not say with any certainty that the latter has definitively superseded the former.

Alongside these two main currents, a third and potentially equally important one has appeared: the force of revolutionary socialism. At present that force remains weaker than the other two, but that may only be because the Dominican Republic is less developed than Chile or Argentina, let us say; and it is likely that in the future, sentiment in favor of a more radical restructuring will grow. Hence, though the Dominican Republic may have passed one hurdle with the restoration in 1978 of democratic government, it is likely that the growth of a more revolutionary challenge to the status quo will produce both increased conflict and polarization *and* call forth a renewed authoritarian response, as in many other of the Latin American countries.

Much depends on the economy. If it continues to expand, the Dominican Republic may be able to continue on a democratic course and head off a revolutionary explosion. But should the economic pie turn stagnant, stop expanding, or even shrink, then the political order will be gravely threatened.

Much also depends on the changing nature of Dominican society. Since Trujillo, the Dominican Republic has become considerably more affluent and considerably more middle class. Some observers argue that these changes militate against future political upheavals because too many Dominicans have too big a stake in things to risk losing all in a major confrontation. We are not sure this new affluence and "middle classness" in the society will produce the stability envisioned. Such changes may raise expectations for even greater change rather than dampening them. And while the middle class may be a force for stability, it is also deeply divided; in defense of its interests, a large sector of the middle class could come to favor a repressive regime.

But the Dominican Republic is changing, and doing so at an accelerated rate. The new affluence, new social programs, the emerging middle class, and economic development are all altering the face of the landscape—physically, psychologically, and politically. Not only are the Dominicans beginning to achieve that place in the sun to which they have always aspired, but what we find particularly interesting and worthwhile are their efforts to diversify their trade and economic relations and thus modify the conditions of dependence under which they have always existed. We are impressed further with their efforts to fashion a political system in accord with *Dominican* desires and traditions, rather than one derived from some foreign source and of questionable appropriateness in the Dominican context.

If the key to breaking out of the interlocking vicious circles of underdevelopment is to attack all of them simultaneously, to modernize the economy while also diversifying, to reduce dependency while also recognizing hard international realities, to solve social problems while also building up capital for investment, and to institutionalize political democracy, but to do so in accord with indigenous values and practices, then the Dominican Republic in the last twenty years seems to have come a considerable distance.

Suggested Readings

Atkins, G. Pope, and Wilson, Larman C. *The United States and the Trujillo Regime* (New Brunswick, N.J.: Rutgers University Press, 1972). A thorough, scholarly study.

Bosch, Juan. *The Unfinished Experiment: Democracy in the Dominican Republic* (New York: Praeger, 1964). An account by the former president.

Crassweller, Robert D. *Trujillo: The Life and Times of a Caribbean Dictator* (New York: Macmillan, 1966). An excellent biography.

Gleijeses, Piero. *The Dominican Crisis: The 1965 Constitutionalist Revolt and the American Intervention* (Baltimore: Johns Hopkins University Press, 1978). Scholarly yet sympathetic to the rebels.

Kryzanek, Michael J. "Political Party Decline and the Failure of Liberal Democracy: the PRD in Dominican Politics," *Journal of Latin American Studies* 9 (1977): 115–43.

———— . "Diversion, Subversion and Repression: The Strategies of Anti-Regime Politics in Balaguer's Dominican Republic," *Caribbean Studies* 19, nos. 1 and 2 (1979). This and the following are among the few serious studies of the Balaguer regime.

———— . "The 1978 Election in the Dominican Republic: Opposition Politics, Intervention and the Carter Administration," *Caribbean Studies*, forthcoming.

Lowenthal, Abraham F. *The Dominican Intervention* (Cambridge: Harvard University Press, 1971). Serious, balanced.

Martin, John Bartlow. *Overtaken by Events: The Dominican Crisis—from the Fall of Trujillo to the Civil War* (Garden City, N.Y.: Doubleday, 1966). Long, fascinating account by a well-meaning U.S. ambassador.

Rodman, Selden. *Quisqueya: A History of the Dominican Republic* (Seattle: University of Washington Press, 1964). Readable but dated.

Sharpe, Kenneth Evan. *Peasant Politics: Struggle in a Dominican Village* (Baltimore: Johns Hopkins University Press, 1977). Good, interesting.

Slater, Jerome. *Intervention and Negotiation: The United States and the Dominican Revolution* (New York: Harper and Row, 1970). The best account of these events.

Walker, Malcolm T. *Politics and the Power Structure: A Rural Community in the Do-
    minican Republic* (New York: Teachers College Press, 1972). An interesting
    case study.
Wiarda, Howard J. *The Dominican Republic: Nation in Transition* (New York:
    Praeger, 1968). An earlier general overview.
_____ . *Dictatorship and Development: The Methods of Control in Trujillo's Domini-
    can Republic* (Gainesville: University of Florida Press, 1970). An analysis of
    the dictatorship.
_____ . *Dictatorship, Development, and Disintegration: Politics and Social Change
    in the Dominican Republic* (Ann Arbor: Xerox University Microfilms Mono-
    graph Series, 1975). Much background and detail.
_____ . and Kryzanek, Michael J. "Dominican Dictatorship Revisited:
    The Caudillo Tradition and the Regimes of Trujillo and Balaguer,"
    Revista/Review Interamericana 7 (Fall, 1977): 417–35. A comparative study.

Index

ABOUT THE AUTHORS

Dr. Howard J. Wiarda is professor of political science, adjunct professor of labor relations, and former chairman of the Program in Latin American Studies at the University of Massachusetts. From 1979 to 1981 he was a visiting scholar at the Center for International Affairs, Harvard University; he has also held a visiting professorship at the Massachusetts Institute of Technology and has been a consultant to the Department of State. He has written and edited numerous papers and books, including *The Continuing Struggle for Democracy in Latin America* (Westview, 1980) and *Corporatism and National Development in Latin America* (Westview, 1981). He was formerly editor of *Polity*, the journal of the Northeast Political Science Association.

Dr. Michael J. Kryzanek is associate professor and chairman of the Department of Political Science at Bridgewater State College in Massachusetts. He earned his doctorate at the University of Massachusetts in 1975; in 1981 he was a visiting researcher at Georgetown University's Latin American Studies Program. His research has been published in the *Journal of Latin American Studies, Caribbean Studies,* and *Revista/Review Inter-Americana;* a chapter "Political Parties, Opposition Politics, and Democracy in Latin America" appeared in the book *The Continuing Struggle for Democracy in Latin America* (Westview, 1980).